MW00633387

Ecological
Architecture

Chris van Uffelen

Ecological
Architecture

BRAUN

CONTENTS

Ecology: House (oikos) and Reasoning (logos)

by Chris van Uffelen

Writing a book about ecological architecture is no easy task – ecology is not a type of building; nor is it a definable style. No ecological solutions could be valid for all climate zones, even if there were a comprehensive canon of technologies honed to perfection. Needless to say, such a canon doesn't exist. Ecological technologies are still evolving, and new products appear on the market each month, whether they are electrical (photovoltaics) or heat (geothermics), insulation (phase change materials) products or building greening techniques. Façade modules can house all necessary building systems or even absorb harmful substances from the air. Which technology is conclusively the right choice for a specific construction task, which combination produces the minimum harm to the environment? These questions have to be answered for each project anew. This book illustrates more than 100 individual cases where dif-ferent approaches have resulted in exemplary ecological structures. In addition to the exploration of progressive technologies, the issue taken up in this field most often is the use and implementation of these in architecture. Many unusual technologies would have to be considered if we don't limit ourselves to architecture and instead take up construction in general. The task of this book, however, is to highlight the interaction of artistic expression and environmentally friendly technology. If just a few years ago photovoltaics were merely installations placed on an opportunely slanted roof, today they have become an integral part of building design – practically every architect implements ecological technologies.

Aesthetic-minded architecture with a concentration on ecology first appeared at the end of the 1960s, but remained solely a stylistic niche. In contrast, many of the technologies that we classify as ecological today have existed from time immemorial. Building with clay is one of the oldest construction techniques, and the use of raw materials (clay, as opposed to baked bricks) has always saved energy. In antiquity, however, energy savings was not a value in itself, but merely a part of the cost-benefit calculation. This is also the case for the practice of recycling building materials and even whole building sections, which was carried out routinely in antiquity and the Middle Ages. Bricks from hypocausts were especially popular due to their strength and standard size.

An existing ancient Roman capitol could be economically adapted to new use and local materials could be found quickly and cheaply, whereas transportation of quality supplies added enormous costs. Four hundred and fourteen ancient Roman columns are found in the Kairouan mosque in Tunisia. Charlemagne let war spoils from Rome and Ravenna be transported over the Alps for his Imperial Palace in Aachen. In this case, recycling came at a high price, but served the political purpose of placing the king as the successor of ancient Roman emperors. The columns' significance can be gathered from the fact that in 1794 they were removed by the French and transported to Paris, and the majority was returned in 1815. Reuse as

↖ | **Elegant Embellishments,** proSolve 370e: three-dimensional air pollution reducing architectural tiles

→ | **Neri Oxman MATERIALECOLOGY,**
Construction In Vivo: osmotic breathable façade
by controlling passive CNT distribution and self-
powered actuation
→→| **Foster + Partners,** 1999, the Reichstag
dome in Berlin: light is guided into the building
using reflection
→→→| **Peter Hübner and Peter Sulzer,** 1980,
Bauhäusle, Stuttgart: student hostel 'Self Build'
↘ | **Photovoltaic panels** on the roof of Pier
Luigi Nervis papal audience hall, Vatican city

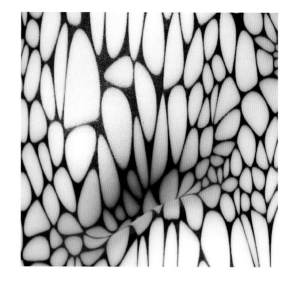

a citation for gaining political legitimacy abated in the Gothic period, as Gothic architecture did not readily accept incorporation of foreign elements. The 145 ancient columns in the atrium behind the western façade of the San Marco cathedral in Venice have lost their load bearing function. Medieval cathedrals also fulfilled the strictest insulation requirements thanks to their structurally necessitated thick walls, successfully keeping bitter cold out of the interior until Easter. These buildings, of course, didn't have heating systems; simple fireplaces and, for large spaces, coal ovens continued to be too much of a rarity during the Early Modern period to present them using special decorative elements as luxury objects.

//

The technical advances in glass manufacture produced larger and cheaper panes, allowing improved illumination with comfortable interior temperatures. During the Renaissance and Baroque periods, dismantling and reuse of antique buildings came into fashion again, reaching a new peak. The columns and capitols corresponded to the current tastes, and the remaining materials were processed into building lime and can-

nonballs. Monument protection, especially for non-ecclesiastical buildings, almost did not exist, while legitimizing spoils (as, for example, during the demolition of the Old St. Peter's Basilica) enjoyed a renewed popularity. A further well-known example is the reuse of stones from the razed Bastille for the Pont de la Concorde, where citizens were given the opportunity to trample the hated prison with their feet.

//

In the context of modern garden architecture, building forms which today would be called ecological came about from grottos and similar covered spaces as well as from the early 'vernacular' style (Hameau de la Reine, Marie-Antoinette's private farm-like retreat in Versailles). By way of the English landscape garden, this romantic architecture continued in the late 19th century as the Arts and Crafts movement which, facing the rise of industrialization, preoccupied itself with manual production, pastoral appearances and natural materials. As next, Art Nouveau brought a nature connection to architecture, albeit often only as decoration: floral elements served as examples of form and ornamentation. In

contrast, during the first decades of the 20th century, rural building methods and natural materials received renewed interest from many perspectives. Going against the grain of Modernism's evolution into the International Style, this movement produced well-known examples such as Ebenezer Howard's garden cities, German Neo-Classicism, which looked back to the period "around 1800", Scandinavian national romanticism and its modern torchbearer found in Hugo Aalto, social consciousness of the Amsterdam School utilizing decorative clinker and thatch roofs, and Frank Lloyd Wright's earth-linked expressionism in Taliesin West. We can nonetheless also find tendencies that we would now describe as ecological among the representatives of geometrical, functional Modernism. As a result of ever increasing information about hygiene (Openlucht School in Amsterdam, Duiker en Bijvoet), daylight and natural illumination were placed at the very core of building design. Elevating buildings allowed soil to remain unsealed to a degree (Corbusier), function analysis allowed reduction of some space programs (Bauhaus) and the

→ | **Françoise-Hélène Jourda & Gilles Perraudin**, 1999, Akademie Mont-Cenis in Herne-Sodingen: buildings in a glasshouse with photo-voltaics
→→| **Jean Nouvel, Emanuel Cattani et Associés**, 1994, Fondation Cartier pour l'Art Contemporain, Paris: extra garden area results from setting the building away from the street
→→→| **Rolf Disch**, 1994, Heliotrop, Freiburg: building rotates toward sunlight
↘ | **Foster + Partners**, 1990, Commerzbank, Frankfurt / Main: gardens for ventilation
↘↘ | **Prof. Jimmy Lim**, Johore Area Rehabilitation, 2008: traditional forms for modern ecology – solids and voids induce more passive movement of air and penetration of light into the building

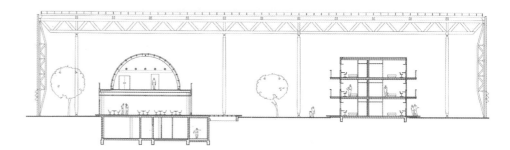

first scientific studies laid the foundation for our current standards (Functionalism). In contrast, the idea of being able to formulate an international architectural vocabulary was not so fortunate for architecture's ecological progress. After WWII, this thinking often led to resource-consuming buildings. Heating and cooling systems were seen as merely providers of comfortable conditions, and not as symptoms of insufficient thermal protection. Energy was cheaper than insulation and materials could be inexpensively transported or manufactured by a quickly developing chemical industry which hardly understood the long term effects of their products.

As the 1960s were coming to a close, factors such as Alexander Mitscherlich's "Unwirtlichkeit unserer Städte" ("Inhospitality of our cities", 1965) and the expansion of the consumer society led to a mounting criticism of its architecture, and an alternative was seen in pre-industrial building methods using natural materials. The search for a Muslim identity beyond the international architectural language led Hassan Fathis (New Barris in Egypt, starting in 1967) to

low-tech architecture. With the rise of the nature conservation movement, and especially following the oil crises of 1974 and 1978, a wide range of consciously ecological low-tech architecture appeared in the 1970s: Peter Huebner, Lucien Kroll, Sverre Fehn and Jourda & Perraudin. Earthen houses were especially popular (Malcom Wells, Gustav Peichl, Arthur Quambie) and sometimes intersected with land art (James Turrell). An analytical-technical perspective was examined with the advance of passive sun energy (Thomas Herzog). In the 1980s, a shift took place towards illustrating mankind's deep-rooted sensitization to the idea of architecture as a counterpart to nature. Examples of this trend are the ironic and provocative Best Stores from SITE, where a tropical rainforest behind flowing water is placed in a shop window or, as in Franz Hohler's story "Die Rückeroberung " ("The Recapture"), plants destroy the walls of a recently completed building. Utopias like James Wine's Highrise of Homes, an assembly of villas inside a multi-storied parking garage, are a provocative statement in protest of landscape-destroying development sprawl. All the time, the influence of the nature

conservation movement was gaining momentum, eventually leading to the rise of the Green Party on Germany's political scene. Architecture at this time was reexamining traditional values: local building materials in critical regionalism (Vorarlberg) and traditional forms in postmodern architecture, whose natural stone dressing often presented only a skin-deep connection to nature. New Urbanism brought back the garden city as a socio-romantic, conservative alternative to cities for the middle class. Ebenezer Howard could not have imagined garden cities without railroad connections to the metropolis, and these settlements were soon transformed into satellite towns, dependent on automobiles. New environmental technologies like improved insulation and solar collectors were developed in the 1980s, and ecological awareness increased rapidly. However, this mind shift started to influence architectural appearance only as the decade came to a close. The first charts comparing key ecological data appeared in the 1990s and for the first time enabled a scientific approach to ecology. Environmental efforts officially became political goals and grew

→ | **Renzo Piano Building Workshop**, 1998,
Jean-Marie Tjibaou Cultural Center, New Caledonia:
bamboo is one of the most ecologically sound construction materials
→→| **Grimshaw & Partners**, 2001, The Eden
Project, Cornwall: each geodesic dome emulates a
natural biome; ETFE is recyclable
↘ | **Jean Nouvel and Patrick Blanc**, 2008,
Musée du quai Branly, Paris: vertical garden

to include the theme of sustainability with
the 1992 United Nations Conference on
Environment and Development held in Rio
de Janeiro. These topics were more suc-
cinctly formulated in the Kyoto Protocol in
1996. Various technologies and processes
got their start in architecture with the sweeping slogan of 'responsibility for today and
tomorrow.' At the forefront were many
hi-tech architects of the 1970s, whose
buildings until this time stood in contrast
to ecological construction methods, but
who were now advocating implementation
of innovative installations and equipment.
Nicholas Grimshaw's English pavilion at the
EXPO '92 in Seville may at first look as if it
consumes profuse amounts of energy by
pumping water over its glazed façades for
cooling purposes, but by using solar power
to fuel this process, it uses a resource readily available in one of Europe's hottest
cities. Such multi-level complex solutions,
photovoltaics and recycling, dominated
sustainable architecture in the 1990s. In
1993, pioneers of ecology such as Norman
Foster, Renzo Piano, Richard Rogers and
Thomas Herzog joined to form the READ
Group (Renewable Energy in Architecture

and Design), which aimed to enforce a
higher standard of low-energy construction
with the support of the European Commis-
sion. In this environment, the demand for
sustainable design became more diversified.
Today's world is unimaginable without
techniques made popular by Norman
Foster's Commerzbank building in Frank-
furt/Main, which features a double glazed
façade acting as climate buffer, complex
building management systems and cross-
ventilation via gardens in high atriums –
a feature, which finds precedent in Ken
Yeang's Sky Courts in Kuala Lumpur,
1989. During the reconstruction of Berlin's
Reichstag, the architect led light inside the
dark building using mirrors situated inside
the glass dome. Simultaneously, a funnel
supporting the dome mirrors draws up air
from the plenary hall out of the building.
Jourda et Perraudin built the continuing
education academy in Herne as an extremely
flexible and practical 'city' under a glass
skin which supports 10,000 square meters
of solar collectors. Another building of
Nicholas Grimshaw, the Eden project,
brings the top three climate zones together
under a thin envelope. Jimmy Lim uses

passed-down knowledge from traditional
building to regulate interior climate and
integrate it into ecological towers with hi-
tech methods. Renzo Piano resorts not only
to historical cone-shaped vernacular structures of Oceania as an inspiration for his
Tjibaou Cultural Center in New Caledonia
which looks like a modernized, monumental
version of a local village, but also utilizes
bamboo, one of the world's most ecological
materials. The DEGW design office significantly reduces space requirements for
office buildings by functional analysis
and implementation of modern production
methods. Michael Sorkin initiates a geo-
morphic city growth as the backbone of a
"Delirious New York." The dawn of the new
millennium brought official recognition to
sustainable architecture with the bestowal
of the Pritzker Prize to Glen Murcutt,
known for his villas using natural building
materials.

All these forms of sustainable architecture,
including those being implemented since
the 1970s or even the Middle Ages, are rep-
resented in this book alongside brand new
21st century technologies. Since global

→ | **Hollwichkushner – HWKN,** 2018, MEtreePOLIS, Atlanta: in 2018 genetic manipulation will allow the integration of a photosynthetic molecular complex with a solid-state electronic device into vegetation, effectively turning modified plants into energy producers
→→| **Jean Nouvel**, 2015, Tour Signal, La Défense: ecological tower
↘ | **Zwarts & Jansma**, AMFORA, planned for 2018, Amsterdam: underground city which would preserve nature surrounding the old town and would cost ca. USD 14.4 billion

warming has been recognized and started being generally accepted as real, a change in paradigm took place in architecture, setting sustainability as a priority above style and structural function. Some ecological characteristics can be easily estimated. These include energy requirements for the manufacture of various construction materials: For sand lime brick, for example, it is 350 kWh/m², for timber 180 kWh/m², and structural steel 57000 kWh/m². But a hi-rise built from timber is not stable, and to construct the enclosed space of a skyscraper in one story will seal too much valuable soil. Co-efficients of heat transmission (U-value) of non-insulated materials are also easily balanced: For a 25-centimeter thick concrete wall, it is 3.3 W/m²K, for a brick layer of similar thickness it is 1.5 W/m²K, while a solid wood wall only 20 centimeters thick has a U-value of 0.5 W/m²K. If windows in such a façade are of double-pane glass, their value is circa 3.0 W/m²K – better than non-insulated concrete. Although it is easy to compare such numbers, it is much harder to draw conclusions from them. Wood has a better heat transmission coefficient, and can be composted after its use; brick, however,

holds with no coating or chemicals and may be easily implemented again. Nonetheless, clay for bricks and wood are not available everywhere. A glass wall eliminates most of the energy needs for illumination. For this reason, almost no international ecological standards have emerged to this day, which may be even a good thing, for while climate control is the focus of improvement in Australia and self-sufficiency is important in low density settlements, in the Netherlands architects are most concerned with soil sealing. Energy can be recovered centrally or reused from waste heat of other buildings. No ecological standards label considers all possible aspects.

Switzerland has the Minergie standard, HQE reigns in France, Denmark has the EPD, while the Netherlands have developed the DCBA and the MEPB ratings; in the United Kingdom the BREEAM serves as the benchmark, while in Europe it is also the CEPMC; CASBEE exists in Japan and for the real estate industry the LEED® rating from the United States is of utmost value. Unfortunately, optical landscape preservation through architectonic conservation or reuse

of untreated metal debris or sand-filled plastic containers has hardly any influence in any of these standards. Although recycling of existing buildings or materials certainly has a positive influence on the energy consumption of building construction, it may demand more energy expenditure in the long term. Energy needed for maintenance, conversion, demolition and recycling, as well as the expected useful life of a building all play a subordinate role in the ecological valuation of a project. There is no definitive way to predict the energy costs for the entire service period of a building. This is where the market finally enters the scene – drastic rise in energy prices during the last decades has forced clients, and with them, the architects, to optimize its utilization.

This book presents buildings that may be called unique in their having been able to find the ideal solution for their situation, and may serve as examples for others. There is no sense in making the search for ecological solutions into a competition, for there can never be a winner. The winner is always our environment.

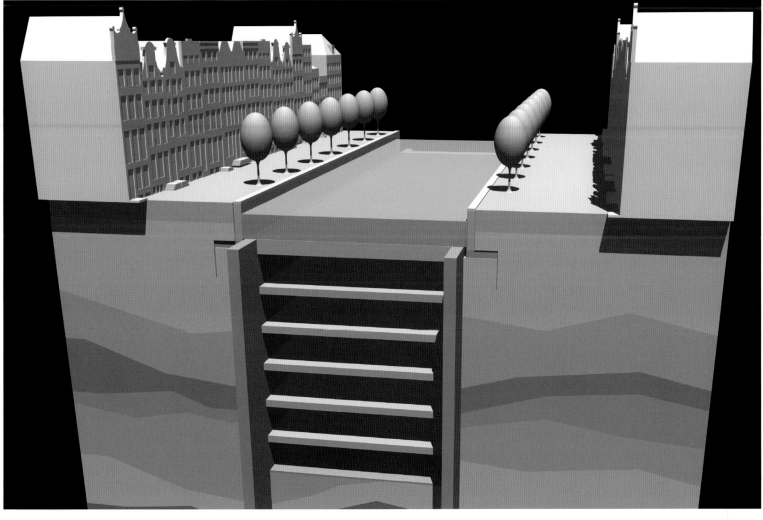

Small

Paul Morgan Architects

↑ | **View** from street
→ | **South view** showing wind scoops

The Cape Schanck House
Victoria

The design was created using computer renderings and wind tunnel tests on a cardboard model and placed within an expanse of smooth native elements – wind forces, vegetal phototropism, diurnal sunlight movement, rain patterns. The form modeling produced an aerodynamic external skin and continuous internal skin. Wind turbulence at the entrance zone resulted in this section of the skin being different. In the living room, the ceiling swings down to an internal water tank. Water is harvested from the entire roof area and is stored in the tank during the summer. The tank cools the ambient air temperature of the living room in warmer months, supplies rain water for toilets and gardening, and structurally carries the roof load.

PROJECT FACTS

Address: 24 Bass Vista Boulevard, Cape Schanck, VIC 3939, Australia. **Client:** Paul and Anna Morgan. **Completion:** 2006. **Ecological aspects:** wind energy; rainwater reuse. **Certificates/standards:** passive energy building.

↑ | **Living room** featuring bulb tank
← | **Front bedroom**
↓ | **Cross section**

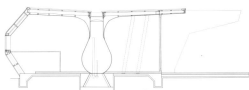

← | **Rear view** from ti tree canopy
↓ | **Ground floor plan**

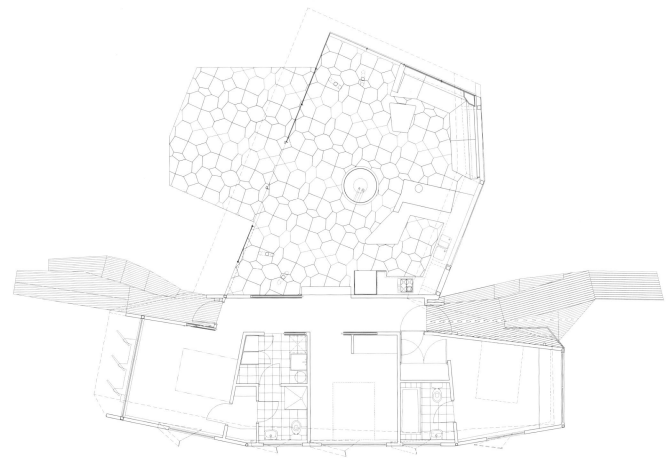

↑ | **View from stream**
↗ | **Front façade summer**
→ | **South elevation** with terraced exterior

Dragspelhuset
Årjäng

This house is an extension of an original cabin dating from the late 1800s, located on the shores of lake Övre Gla in the Glaskogen nature reserve in Sweden. To maximize their possibilities, the designers created an extension that is capable of evolving. The building can literally adjust itself to its environment depending on the weather or the number of occupants. During the winter, the building is a cocoon with protection against the cold in the form of a double skin which unfurls in the summer like a butterfly. The organic shape of the house of red cedar wood naturally blends into the forest setting. Following the tradition of the Sami tribe, reindeer hides are used in the interior as insulation. The house is an almost CO_2-free design.

PROJECT FACTS

Address: Kopparebäcken, Smolmark 67293 Årjäng, Sweden. **Client:** Family Zeisser. **Completion:** 2004. **Ecological aspects:** solar energy, running water directly from the stream; three wood stoves, including one for the bathtub; rainwater reuse; composting outhouse; no maintenace due to untreated cedar wood. **Degree of sealing:** 3%. **Certificates/standards:** zero energy building.

← | **Interior view** from the dining table
↙ | **Interior view** of the kitchen

↑ | **Front façade,** winter at dusk
↙ | **Ground floor plan** moved together
↓ | **Ground floor plan** expanded

GRAFT
Gesellschaft von Architekten

↑ | Bird's-eye view

Bird Island

Kuala Lumpur

The designers applied an integrated strategy for developing a zero energy building that seamlessly dovetails the economic and sustainable advantages of environmentally friendly living with the needs of a demanding, cosmopolitan clientele. While providing an expansive outdoor living deck, the primary living space is concentrated inside cooled zones. A maximum amount of energy-efficient floor area is created and sheltered from the elements by a dynamic tensile structure. The traditional relationship between indoor and outdoor has been shifted, allowing for comfort that is freed from the bonds of traditional walls. When possible, almost all materials chosen were renewable or recycled.

Address: Sentul Park, Kuala Lumpur, Malaysia. **Client:** YTL Land Development. **Completion:** 2010. **Ecological aspects:** solar, wind energy; 100% renewable energy from heat pumps, photovoltaic plant; minimized footprint; local plants (pest prevention), stones; tent structure from engineered bamboo; bamboo flooring; solar heat; transmission heat loss $U = 0.1$ W/m²K (walls); insulation glazing $U = 0.6$ W/m²K; rainwater reuse; ventilation engineering. **Certificates/standards:** zero energy building, LEED Platinum (candidate).

BIRD ISLAND
participant number 8
site number 1

↑ | **Plan**
↓ | **Front elevation**

↑ | **View from lakeside**

Kengo Kuma & Associates

↑ | **Entrance** on west side
→ | **East elevation**

Y-Hutte

East Japan

The naturalistic concept of the building is the result of reflection on what a hut in the forest should be like. The form is structured by three panels resting on each other, producing a triangular pyramid. The panels with wood ribs, separated by small pitches, act as both walls and roof. They filter daylight similarly to forest foliage. The slanted panels converge at the top, giving an impression of branches that have been tied together. The house recalls a primitive ancient hut that has been furnished with 21st century comforts and perfectly integrated into its surroundings due to its "close to nature" approach.

PROJECT FACTS

Address: confidential, Japan. **MEP engineer:** P.T.Morimura & Associates. **Client:** private. **Completion:** 2006. **Ecological aspects:** heat reservoir; the air layer is added to the insulation of the styrofoam; insulation glazing of Low-E double glass; ventilation engineering; weather resistance of wood improved by alkaline copper quaternary. **Degree of sealing:** 7%. **Certificates/standards:** low/passive energy building.

←←| **View of ground floor** and gallery
← | **Bathroom**
↙ | **Ground floor plan**
↓ | **Section**

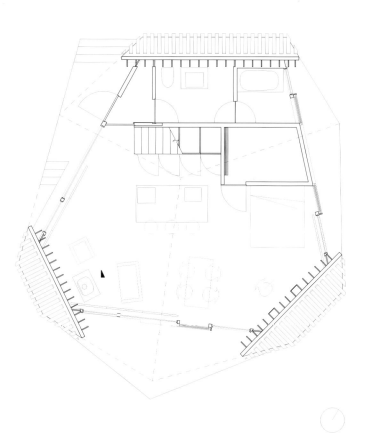

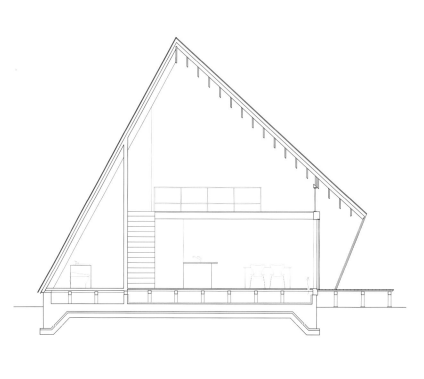

Labics,
Centola & Associati/Luigi
Centola

↑ | **Underground parking** and new houses

Underground Parking, River Remodeling & Social Housing

City of Amalfi

This project is part of a superordinate renaturalization masterplan sited in the magnificent context of the Amalfi Coast Unesco site. The project's approach is to recover a set of neglected pre-industrial water mills. In order to allow only eco-friendly access to the site, an underground parking area was designed, encouraging visitors to explore the site by foot. A water powered elevator connects the parking lot and the lower public path near the river with the upper public path. Further, more small social housing estates were erected to replace the former incoherent settlements.

PROJECT FACTS

Address: Canneto Valley, City of Amalfi, Italy. **Client:** City of Amalfi. **Completion:** 2012. **Ecological aspects:** solar energy, micro-hydroelectrical energy from the river; solar heat; thermo-active building systems; regrowing wood (lemon pergolas); rainwater reuse; recovering of existing water channels and lemon terraces. **Certificates/standards:** low energy building.

↑ | Bird's-eye view
↓ | Section

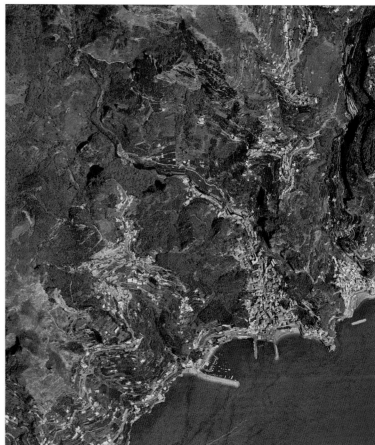

↑ | Site plan

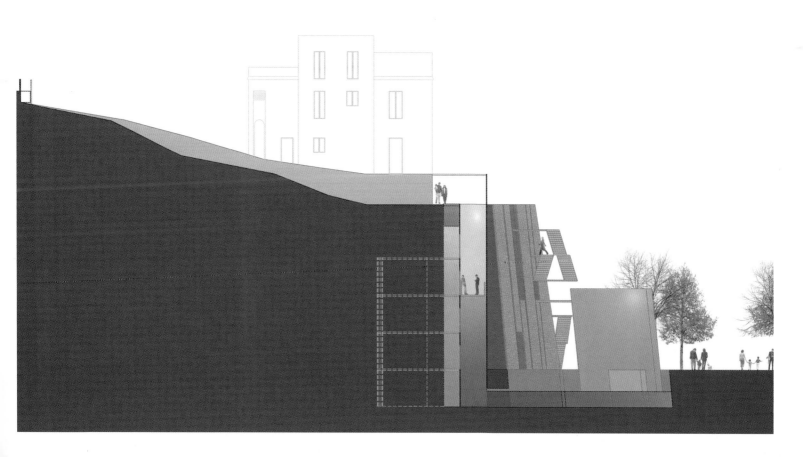

Peter Kuczia

↑ | **South elevation**
→ | **South-west elevation**
→→| **Detail of wood panelled façade**

CO_2 Saver House

Laka

This house located on Lake Laka blends in with its surrounding landscape. Colorful panels set into the timber façade reflect the tones of the country site. The outer countenance of the building is symmetrical, whereas the interior violates the symmetrical order following the functional requirements of the space. In addition to aesthetic considerations, the form was chosen for optimization of solar energy absorbance. The ground floor was externally clad with untreated larch boarding, and a set-in glazed patio was integrated to gain solar energy. Additional solar collection panels were mounted on the roof and a ventilation plant with a thermal recovery system ensures energy cost reduction for heating and lighting.

PROJECT FACTS

Address: Piotra Skargi 31, 43–241 Laka, Poland. **Client:** Peter and Dorota Kuczia. **Completion:** 2008. **Ecological aspects:** solar energy; solar heat; heat recovery; recycled aggregate; regrowing wood; transmission heat loss $U = 0.14$ W/m²K (walls); airtight; insulation glazing $U = 1.0$ W/m²K; winter garden 16 m² glass; rainwater reuse; ventilation engineering; 70 m² covered with green. **Degree of sealing:** 6.5 %. **Certificates/standards:** low energy building.

↖ | **The "Black box"**
↑ | **Different claddings**
↙ | **Plans,** ground floor plan and section

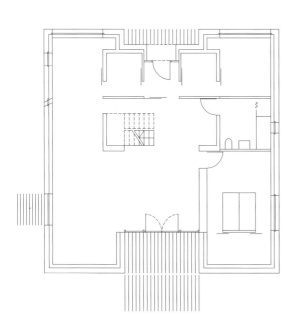
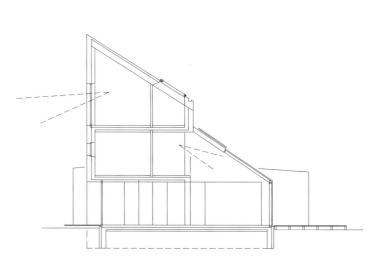

← | Untreated larch wood cladding
↓ | Drawings

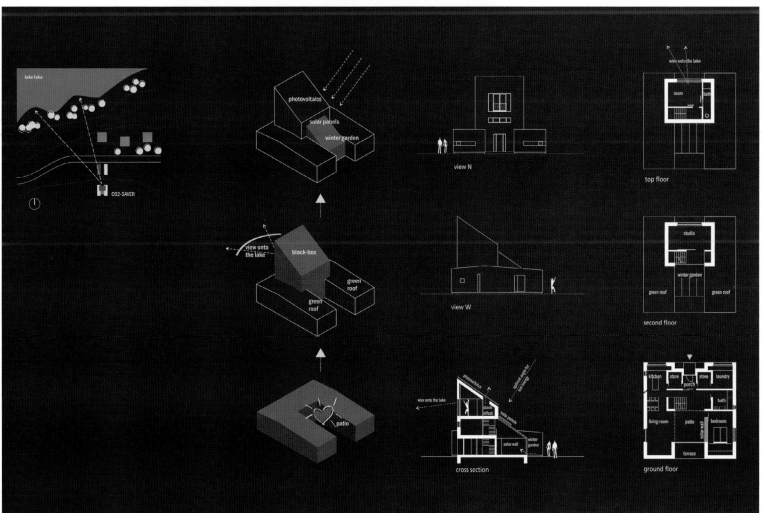

Turf Design Studio

↑ | Wall detail

Salad Bar

Cronulla

The Salad Bar was featured at the 2004 Built Environment Future Gardens exhibition in the Royal Botanic Gardens in Sydney. The exhibition demonstrated how environmental sustainability could be practically incorporated into contemporary living. In 2005, the Salad Bar was invited to join the Houses of the Future exhibition held at Sydney Olympic Park. The project provides a modular vertical growing structure with a footprint that is smaller than a generic garden, enabling it to occupy small spaces. Integrating a 'bar' within the vegetated wall provides a playful vision of how self sufficiency can be incorporated into contemporary urban living.

PROJECT FACTS

Address: 95 The Kingsway, Cronulla, NSW 2230, Australia. **Planning partner:** Co-Ordinated Land-scapes, Elmich Australia. **Client:** Turf Design Studio. **Completion:** 2004. **Ecological aspects:** vegetation harnesses sun's energy for human consumption; thermoactive building systems; recycled hardwood timber; regrowing and regenerating plant material; rainwater reuse; complete building automation; 65 m² covered with green; **Certificates/standards:** AILA Award.

↑ | **Vertical gardens,** the sky is the limit
↓ | **Design** for park context

↑ | **Children in front of the fresh salad**

Pugh + Scarpa Architects

↑ | **South elevation,** view into the living area and balcony at ground level
→ | **Solar canopy** and sun deck

Solar Umbrella

Santa Monica

This home was built as a residence for the principals of the architects' office and their young son. Sustainability was the project's top priority, setting responsible living in the 21st century as its goal. Inspired by Paul Rudolph's Umbrella House of 1953, the Solar Umbrella provides a contemporary reinvention of the solar canopy that provides thermal protection in climates with intense exposures by using photovoltaic panels to cover 100 % of the home's energy needs. In addition to the photovoltaic solar panel array, the home's green aspects include solar hydronic heating panels, a storm-water retention system, and an airy, open design.

PROJECT FACTS

Address: 2525 Michigan Avenue, Building F1, Santa Monica, CA 90404, USA. **Client:** Angela Brooks & Lawrence Scarpa. **Completion:** 2005. **Ecological aspects:** solar energy; 73% renewable energy; solar heat; recycled fly-ash concrete, cold-rolled steel; insulation glazing, thermal breaks in aluminum window frames; glass air conditioning, skin double glazed krypton filled Low-E windows with stainless steel spacers; rainwater reuse. **Degree of sealing:** 35%. **Certificates/standards:** ASHRAE Standard 2001, California Title 24.

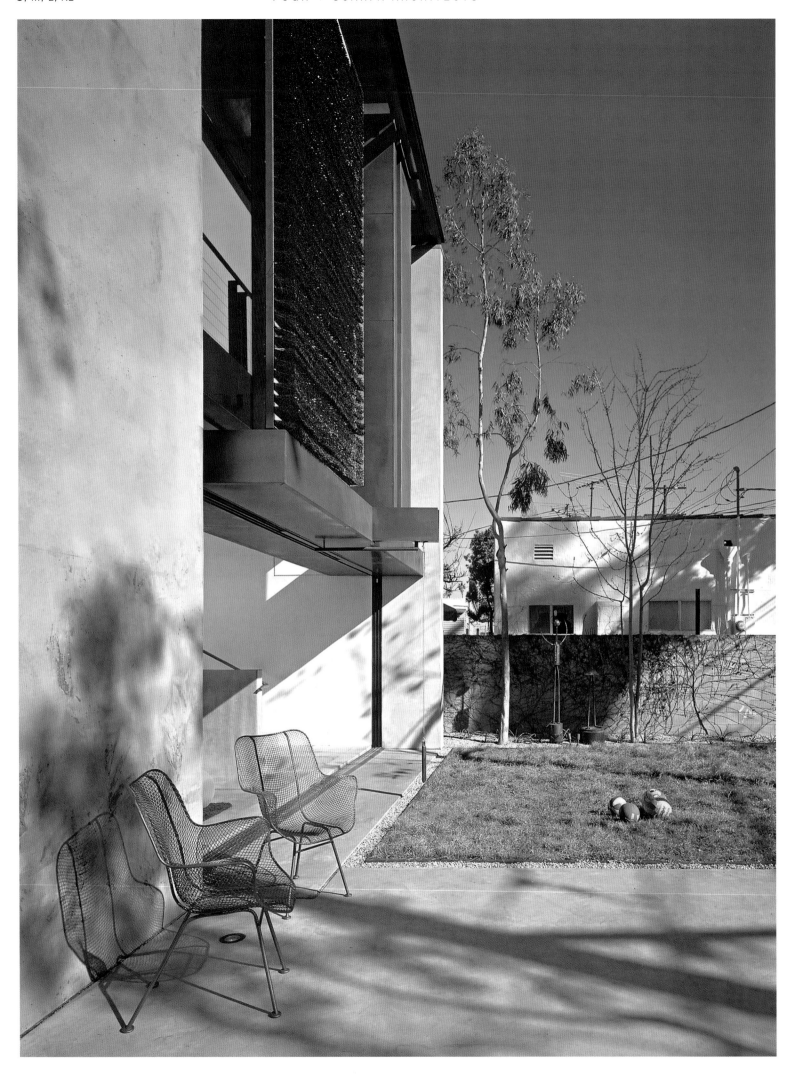

←← | **Lawn and living room** facing north-east
← | **Kitchen**
↓ | **Sketch** of solar panel umbrella concept

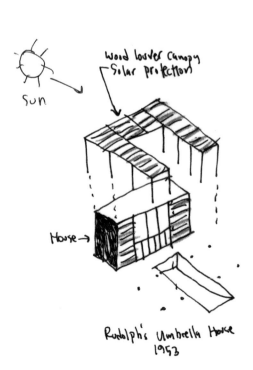

Rudolph's Umbrella House
1953

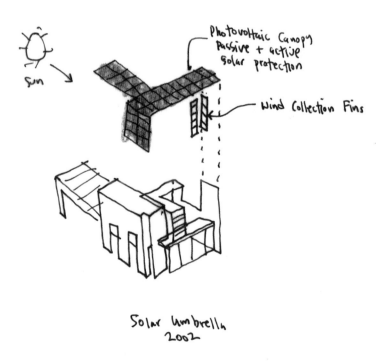

Solar Umbrella
2002

sander architects

↑ | **View from street side,** entrance and staircases
→ | **East view,** corkscrew stairs and balcony

Tree House

Wilmington

The house on a cul-de-sac at the end of a mature subdivision was designed for the sister of the architect. Due to restrictions imposed by the Army Corps of Engineers and the risk of flooding, the building is designed as a vertical house, with a raised living room and master suite. Being in these spaces give one the feeling of being up in a tree. Horizontal windows encircle the house, providing select views into the landscape. In contrast to these small views, a great wrap-around window in the double-height living room provides a dominant diagonal focus for the house, and leads views into the deep woods lying to the northeast.

PROJECT FACTS

Address: Wilmington, DE, USA. **Structural engineer:** Gregg Grubin, CSWST2. **Client:** Leslie Sander. **Completion:** 2006. **Ecological aspects:** heat exchanger; high-density insulating walls and skin; recycled wood studs and beams, bamboo floors; low-VOC paints; high-efficiency lighting; regrowing wood.

↖ | **North-west view,** garage
← | **South-west view,** entry

← | **Interior view**, living room
↓ | **First floor plan**

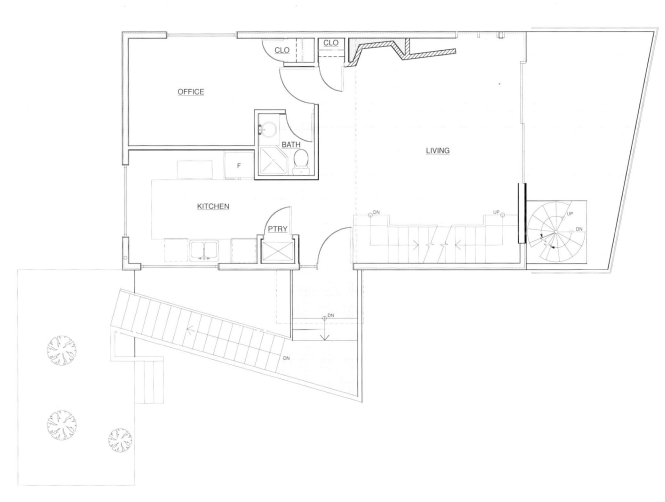

Kjellgren Kaminsky
Architecture

↑ | **Exterior perspective**

Villa Värde

anywhere

The architects have developed Sweden's first series of prefabricated houses with passive house technique. The goal is to make this technique available to anyone, demonstrating that low energy houses and good architecture can go hand in hand. The name of the project means Villa Value, and the goal was to give customers the most villa for their money. The plan is compact and functional, making the most of its 120 square meters. The living room is nonetheless spacious and has double-height ceilings. The double height can be also transformed into two extra bedrooms if desired.

PROJECT FACTS

Address: N/A. **Client:** Emrahus. **Completion:** 2010. **Ecological aspects:** solar energy; solar heat (70% of needs); heat exchanger (reuses 80% indoor air); transmission heat loss: U=0.1 W/m²K (walls), U=0.08 W/m²K (roof), U=0.08 W/m²K (floor), U=0.76 W/m²K (windows). **Certificate/standards:** Swedish passive house standard.

↑ | **Living room**
↓ | **Barbecue** and housewarming party

↓↓ | **Plans**, first and second floor
↓↓ | **Passive house principle**

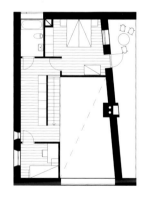

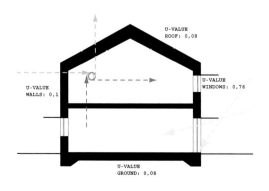

U-VALUE ROOF: 0,08
U-VALUE WALLS: 0,1
U-VALUE WINDOWS: 0,76
U-VALUE GROUND: 0,08

Jens J. Ternes, Architekt BDA,
Architekten + Ingenieure

↑ | **South-west view**
→ | **South view**

Office Building

Koblenz

The tectonic building is an exciting prelude of a ring-shaped development arment along the edge of the square surrounded by older buildings. The horizontally accented, light attic levitates above the massive reinforced concrete cube. The highly insulated envelope is variably shaded by an external sun shade on the aluminum façade. Non-load bearing inner walls and building planning aimed at sustainability enable the house to be reprogrammed in the future. Rated with a Class A energy efficiency, the house is equipped with variable ventilation and floor heating operated using an air-water heat pump.

PROJECT FACTS

Address: Schulgasse 2, 56073 Koblenz, Germany. **Planning partner:** Christian Freund. **MEP engineer:** Fraunhofer Institut Duisburg. **Client:** Jens J. Ternes. **Completion:** 2006. **Ecological aspects:** solar energy; 40 % renewable energy; solar heat; heat exchanger, pumps, recovery; transmission heat loss $U=0.35$ W/m²K; airtight BlowerDoor; insulation glazing $U=1.1$ W/m²K; ventilation engineering; arid urinal. **Degree of sealing:** 77 %. **Certificates/standards:** low/passive energy building.

↑ | **Entrance area**
← | **Staircase**
↓ | **Sketch**

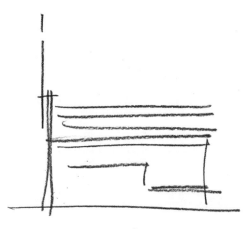

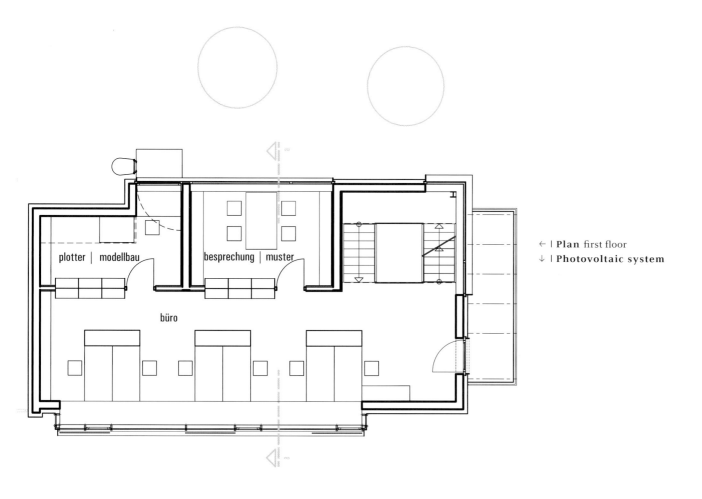

plotter | modellbau

besprechung | muster

büro

← | **Plan** first floor
↓ | **Photovoltaic system**

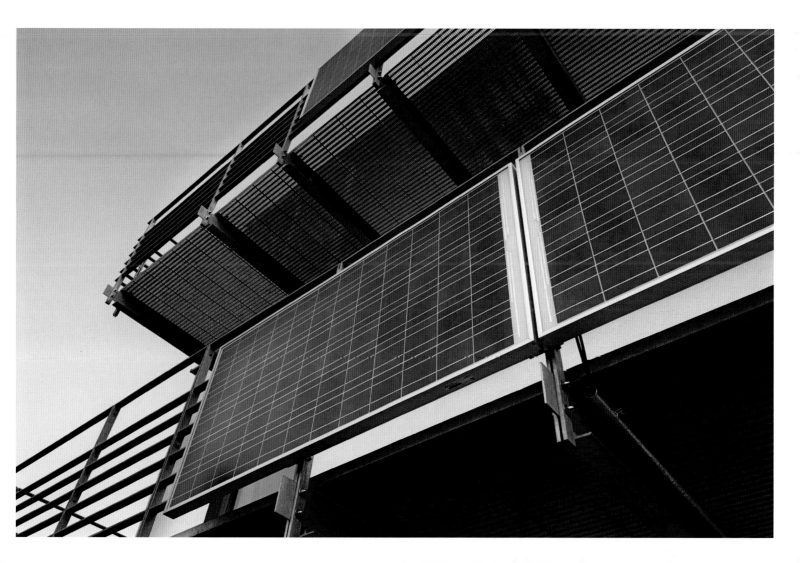

Obie G. Bowman

↑ | **Main house,** cantilevered loft with north
coastline beyond

Oregon Coast Vacation House
Gold Beach

Both buildings anchor themselves to the site with Port Orford cedar log exoskeletons
inspired by the driftwood logs found along the rocky shoreline. Main house heat gain is
controlled by tinted recessed glazing, interior shades, and passive ventilation exhaust-
ing hot air at the apex of the interiors. The off-grid garden house is used as a writing
studio, green house, and guest house. Its compact footprint reduces energy (and most
other) requirements for the building. Domestic water holding tanks are filled by solar
powered pumps from a shallow well and a rooftop condensation and rainwater collection
system. Landscaping is a regeneration of existing vegetation except for a lavender bed to
the west.

PROJECT FACTS

Address: Gold Beach, OR 97444, USA. **Client:** private. **Completion:** 2006. **Ecological aspects:** solar energy; solar heat (garden house); heat reservoir, exchanger; recycled slat siding, railroad tie retaining walls, redwood gutter; transmission heat loss $U=0.057$ (walls), $U=0.033$ (roofs); Low-E insulated, tinted glass; rainwater reuse; ventilation engineering. **Degree of sealing:** 74%. **Certificates/standards:** low energy building (main house), passive/zero energy building (garden house).

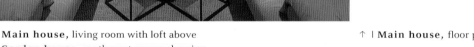

↑ | **Main house,** living room with loft above
↓ | **Garden house,** south-west corner showing
integrated solar panels

↑ | **Main house,** floor plan

H Arquitectes /
David Lorente, Josep Ricart,
Xavier Ros, Roger Tudó

↑ | **View from below**
→ | **West façade**

House 205

Barcelona

Removal of the top layer of earth exposed a wide rock bank capable of supporting a house. Earth movement was minimized and the uniqueness of the location and the existing natural layout was preserved in order to provide access to the garden and to conserve the features of the forest and its flora. The construction uses wooden load bearing walls with a frame system to unite the structure and carpentry. The system of equally sized, flexible use rooms works as a diffuse structure with neither a hierarchy nor a Cartesian organization of load bearing walls. Cut in a factory workshop using a numeric control cutting method, the frame is highly accurate.

PROJECT FACTS **Address:** Calle dels pinetons, parcel·la8, 08233 Vacarisses, Barcelona, Spain. **Planning partner:** Montse Fornés Guàrdia, Miguel Ángel Rodríguez Nevado. **Cybernetics:** Artur Gispert. **Interior architect:** Toni Jiménez Anglès. **Client:** Francesc Ortega, Maria Ferriol. **Completion:** 2008. **Ecological aspects:** solar heat; transmission heat loss U=0.46 W/m²K, insulation glazing U=2.00 W/m²k; cover inertia; rainwater reuse. **Degree of sealing:** 3.3%.

↑ | **Exterior view**
↙ | **Plan,** double glazing façade

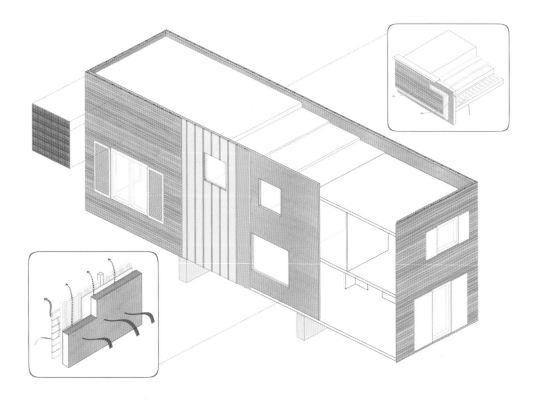

← | **Interior view,** study
↙ | **Interior view,** first floor
↓ | **Heat image,** façade

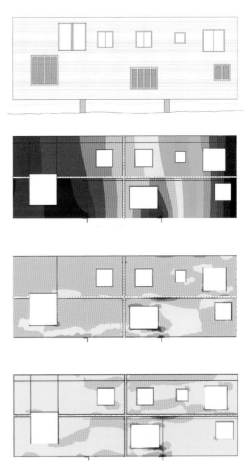

DeSo – Defrain Souquet
Architects,
Christine Dalnoky Land-
scape Architect

↑ | Aerial view

Ocher Mines Bruoux

Gargas

The building under a wooden trellis unites all common features of entrance facilities like
a ticket desk, shop, sanitary units and a refreshment stall. Its orientation responds to the
geographical situation and protects it from the dominant western wind. The outer walls
with an openwork wood façade do not just echo the vertical rhythm of the trees, but also
work as a filter for the rising sun. A wall in natural and ocher-colored concrete is positioned against a hill. It constitutes the technical area, including patios that diffuse natural
light and a vegetal roof. The wall and the hill are the backbone of the thermoactive system
connected to the technical area.

PROJECT FACTS

Address: route d'ocre Oroagnes, 84400 Gargas, France. **Planning partner:** Nathalie Capelli. **Client:** Ville de Gargas. **Completion:** 2008. **Ecological aspects:** thermo-active building systems; natural ventilation; recycled local wood; earth insulation; ventilation engineering; roof, walls covered with green.

↑ | **View by night**
↓ | **Plans,** entrance area ground floor plan and roof

↓ | **Wood structure**

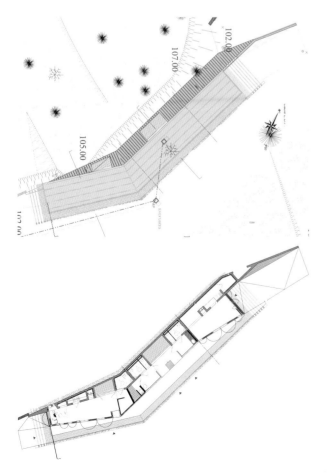

↑ | **Entrance area**
↗ | **Exterior view towards south-west**
→ | **Covered waiting area**

Kielder Observatory

Northumberland

The design of this astronomical observatory sited in a remote spot in Northumberland, close to Scotland, in an area with a very low level of light pollution, envisions a building in the form of a land pier that is able to house two telescopes and a warm-room used for research activities. Timber was chosen as the main material because of its relation to the surrounding forest and its carbon neutrality. The power strategy was developed with a local renewables specialist and encompasses a 2.5 kilowatt wind turbine which utilizes the windy weather conditions of the site for operating power needs, and photovoltaic panels to power deep cell batteries.

PROJECT FACTS

Address: Kielder Water and Forest Park, Northumberland, United Kingdom. **Client:** Kielder Partnership. **Completion:** 2008. **Ecological aspects:** solar, wind energy; 100% renewable energy; entirely self-powered; excess power from wind turbine for heating; regrowing wood; insulation glazing Low-E double glazed roof lights; composting WC. **Certificates/standards:** zero energy building.

↑ | **Exterior view** facing east
← | **View along the corridor**

← | **Photovoltaic panels** on the roof
↓ | **Ground floor plan**
↓↓ | **Sketch**

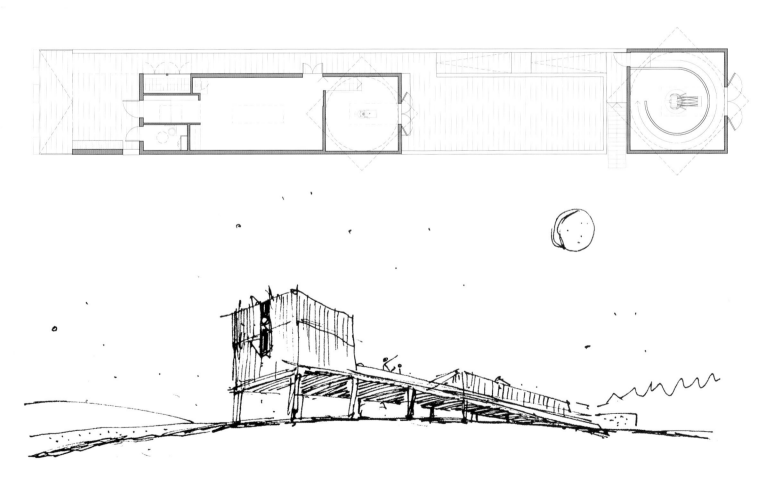

Meixner-Schlüter-Wendt
Architekten

↑ | **New church wall** with new court
→ | **Exterior view**

Dornbusch Church
Frankfurt/Main

The 60-year-old church in a residential area was in poor condition and there was discussion of a complete demolition and construction of a small new "prayer room." However, planning studies gave evidence that a partial demolition was the best solution. The new building is 350 square meters smaller than the original, but remains a spatially and functionally intact ensemble. The spacious area around the altar and the choir was kept, while the opposite side was closed with a new façade. This wall is marked with outlines and moulds of the "old" church, sculpting the flat surface. The outlines of the demolished church are marked on the churchyard.

PROJECT FACTS

Address: Mierendorfstraße 5, 60320 Frankfurt/Main, Germany. **Structural engineer:** Dipl. Ing. Hans Gruhn. **Client:** Evangelischer Regionalverband Frankfurt. **Completion:** 2005. **Ecological aspects:** recycled demolition waste; conversion of unused buildings/monuments because of dismantling/rehabilitation of remaining elements of the old church; upgrade and adjustment to current needs; avoiding producing construction debris. **Degree of sealing:** 26%.

↑ | **Interior view**
↙ | **Site plan**

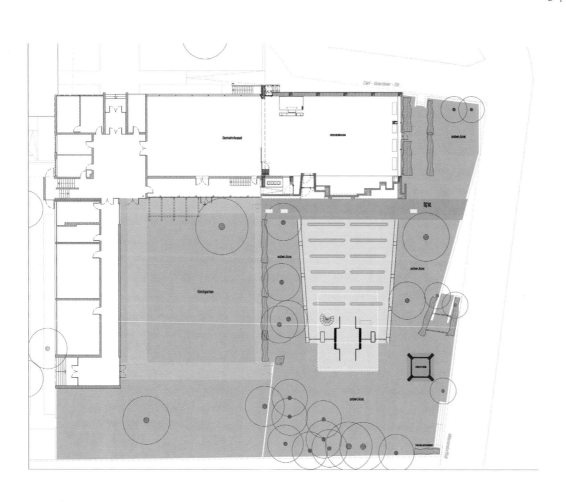

← | **Mold of the old church,** outside and inside
↓ | **Interior of the church hall**

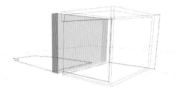

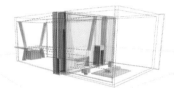
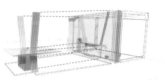

sander architects

↑ | **Atrium,** family cube
→ | **Main room**

Canal House
Venice, CA

The house is composed of three cubes: an elevated mass facing the street acts as a studio, and two other volumes orient to the canal and house the residential program. The design aims to set an opposition between the two sections. The building and its fenestration are sited to maximize passive heating and cooling. Horizontal rusted steel fins provide shade to prevent heat gain in high summer. Vertical rusted steel fins are angled to direct onshore breezes from the nearby ocean into the house. Within both volumes, surfaces have been folded, warped, wrapped, and while there are few interior walls per se, space is divided sufficiently, both horizontally and vertically, to allow place and hierarchy. Minimal landscaping with native plants minimizes water usage.

PROJECT FACTS

Address: Venice, CA, USA. **Client:** private. **Completion:** 2003. **Ecological aspects:** floor radiant heat, on-demand water heater; multi-cell acrylic panels (with high R-value) for glazing reduces heat loss/gain; steel fins provide shade and control ventilation; recycled concrete; regrowing bamboo (flooring); ventilation engineering; low-flush toilets. **Degree of sealing:** 87%.

↑ | **Floor and stairs** covered with bamboo
← | **Bedroom**

← | **Exterior view** by night
↓ | **Plans,** loft plan and first floor plan

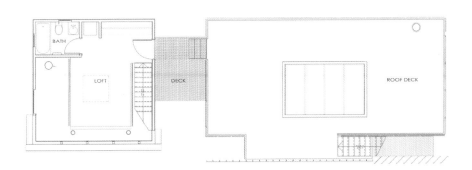

Bucholz McEvoy Architects

↑ | **Side elevation**
→ | **Canopy**

Two Pavilions at Leinster House
Dublin

The Pavilions at Leinster House are designed to provide an open and welcoming entrance to the Government Buildings, expressing the open and transparent manner with which government is conducted. Further approaches were to secure both members and the public unobtrusively and seamlessly, enhancing security and maximizing the beauty of the forecourt to the Government Buildings, and in particular the existing plane trees. In order to achieve these objectives, two simple glass pavilions have been designed to streamline the process of entering. The new entry is composed of three parts: the renovated vehicular entry, the glass entry pavilion, and the refurbished stone exit pavilion.

PROJECT FACTS

Address: Leinster House Forecourt, Government Buildings, Kildare Street, Dublin 2, Ireland. **Client:** Office of Public Works. **Completion:** 2008. **Ecological aspects:** solar energy; solar heat, providing local microclimate control to building occupant; passive solar heating via glazing, passive solar shading using tree cover; natural ventilation via manual and mechanised openings, thermostatic control. **Certificates/standards:** AAI Award, RIAI Award, Mies van der Rohe Award (candidate).

←← | **Side elevation**
← | **Interior view**, security check
↓ | **Site plan**, Leinster Pavilion and Siopa
Pavilion
↓↓ | **Front elevation**, Leinster Pavilion and
Siopa Pavilion

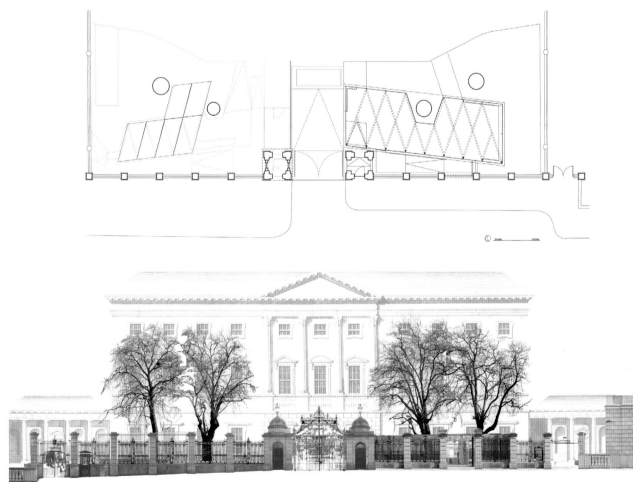

Shubin + Donaldson
Architects

↑ | **Front elevation** with entrance area
→ | **Entrance area** during night

Riviera Residence
Santa Barbara

The house is designed to open up to the outdoors. By taking up minimal space for maximum use, the project also consumes a minimum of resources. It embraces further characteristics of environmentally sustainable design, like reusing existing foundation and caissons, a passive rooftop solar heating system which provides domestic hot water and a passive solar ground-level hot water system to heat the pool. The natural flow of hot and cool air is fortified by the use of radiant hot water floor heating and separate central air conditioning in the ceilings. Although these systems are in place, they are rarely used thanks to the home's solar orientation and natural ventilation.

PROJECT FACTS

Address: Santa Barbara, CA, USA. **Landscaping:** Lane Goodkind. **Interior design:** Genie Gable Interior Design. **Client:** Geoffrey Moore, Genie Gable. **Completion:** 2006. **Ecological aspects:** solar energy; solar heat; hydronic floor heating; re-used existing foundation and caissons; insulation glazing; solar orientated siting; ventilation engineering.

←← | **Living room,** coastline view
↙↙ | **Exterior view** at twilight
← | **Corridor** and bathroom
↓ | **Elevations**
↓↓ | **Plans,** ground floor plan and first floor plan

↑ | **Entrance area** with carport
→ | **Courtyard,** residential building and corridor

House Widen
Grabs

The geometrically plain form of the single-family home has a clear vocabulary, which perfectly assimilates to the architectonic milieu of its location. The two-story residential building cube stands at the center and is clasped by the addition. Untreated wood was predominantly used as the building material with addition of clay as plaster. Thanks to the compact structural form with a well insulated outer façade and south orientation, thermal energy can be used in highly efficient ways. In addition, a brine/water heat pump, controlled building ventilation and geothermal probes lowered to 120 meters have been installed. Space heating and hot water generation take place exclusively via the heat pump.

PROJECT FACTS

Address: 9472 Grabs, Switzerland. **Energy concept:** Lenum AG. **MEP engineer:** ITW Ingenieurunter-
nehmung AG. **Client:** private. **Completion:** 2008. **Ecological aspects:** geothermal energy; brine-water
heat pump; regrowing wood, clay plaster; ventilation engineering. **Certificates/standards:** Minergie-P.

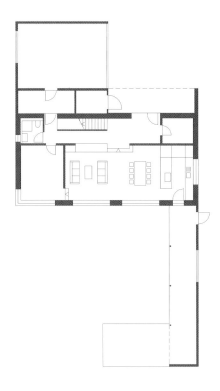

↖ | **Staircase**
← | **Corridor,** first floor
↑ | **Ground floor plan**
↓ | **First floor plan**

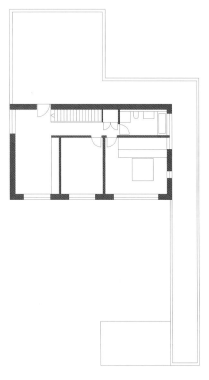

← | **Interior view,** kitchen and dining room
↓ | **Elevations**

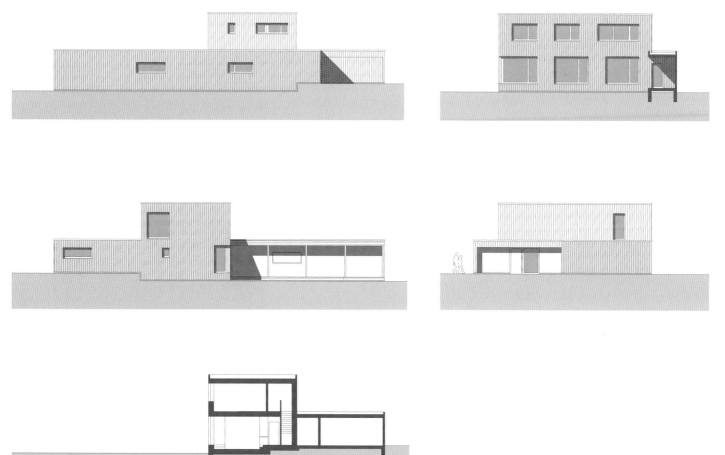

Lindsay Johnston

↑ | **Exterior view**
→ | **Entrance area**

House at Cramond

Edinburgh

Cramond is a village with a traditional architecture of stone houses with clipped eaves, steep slate gabled roofs and white render. The challenge to design a house that would be a modern interpretation of the traditional vernacular language of the region and would also explore new environmental strategies and technologies was met with detailed glass-to-glass corner windows, dormers, balconies, canopies and decks and by introducing a solar conservatory on the south end to capture passive solar gain. The highly insulated SIPS system was used with the walls and roof construction resembling a big box of rigid lightweight insulated panels consisting of polystyrene sandwiched between layers of particle board.

PROJECT FACTS

Address: confidential, Edinburgh, United Kingdom. **Planning partner:** Scott Wardlaw. **Structural engineer:** Philip Thomson and Partners, SIPS Industries. **Client:** private. **Completion:** 2003. **Ecological aspects:** solar, geothermal, energy; solar heat; heat reservoir, exchanger, pumps, recovery; thermo-active building systems; boreholes; transmission heat loss saves 1.67 tons CO_2/year; insulation glazing SIPS system; rainwater reuse; ventilation engineering.

↑ | **Photovoltaic system** on the roof
← | **Detail,** balcony structure

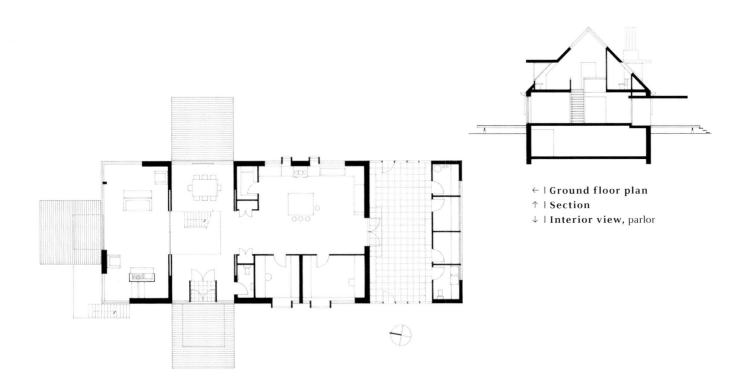

← | **Ground floor plan**
↑ | **Section**
↓ | **Interior view**, parlor

Todd Saunders

↑ | **Exterior view,** folded structure creating
the impression of larger dimensions
↗ | **Exterior,** kitchen
→ | **Perspectives**
→→| **Exterior,** bedroom

Summer House
Åland

Due to the site's constraints, the architects were forced to develop a small building. Its long, continuous, folded structure has an effect of making the house appear larger than its actual size. All rooms can be connected and separated through sliding glass doors – a flexible space concept that allows the use of every single square meter for diverse functions. Not only is the limited space treated responsibly, but the environment is taken into consideration as well. The house is insulated with woven linseed fiber and all wood components, made using material purchased from a local sawmill, are protected with cold pressed linseed oil. The house itself is built on pillars in order to preserve the natural landscape.

PROJECT FACTS

Address: Åland, Finland. **Planning partner:** Tommie Wilhelmsen. **Client:** M.Bauer. **Completion:** 2003.
Ecological aspects: linseed fiber insulation; linseed oil wood treatment. **Degree of sealing:** 12%.
Certificates/standards: passive energy building.

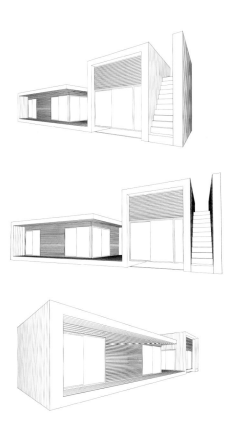

↑ | **Porches** with light rack
→ | **South skylight** for harvesting light

Solar Direct Yield House Zihl
Beinwil am See

House Zihl is the result of a comprehensive approach to architecture, construction ecology, biology and energy use. The plot with a slightly titled south cliff and a completely open horizon enabled extensive room and water heating utilizing the sun's rays. Solar energy deficiency during the winter months makes them the critical period for the solar house. In the months of November to January, a wood oven is needed to maintain comfortable inner temperature if cloudy weather or fog persist. According to calculations, one cubic meter of beech wood is consumed during a heating period.

PROJECT FACTS

Address: Vorderes Zihl 5, 5712 Beinwil am See, Switzerland. **Planning partner:** Andrea Gustav Rüedi. **Client:** Anja and Daniel Huber-Stollberg. **Completion:** 2008. **Ecological aspects:** solar energy; 100% renewable energy; heat recovery; thermo-active building systems; regrowing cellulose insulation; transmission heat loss $Q_t = 182$ MJ/m²a; airtightness $n_{50,st} = 0.33$ [h-1]; 229 m² green covered. **Degree of sealing:** 11%. **Certificates/standards:** passive energy building, solar direct yield house, Minergie-P.

↑ | Terrace and balcony
← | Ground floor plan

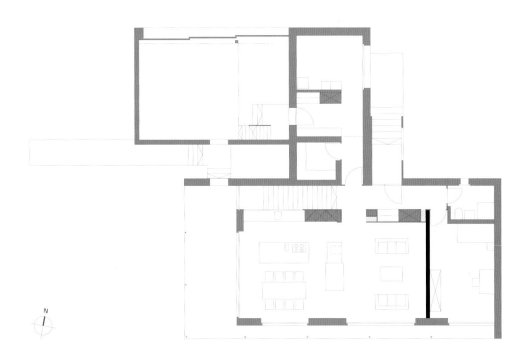

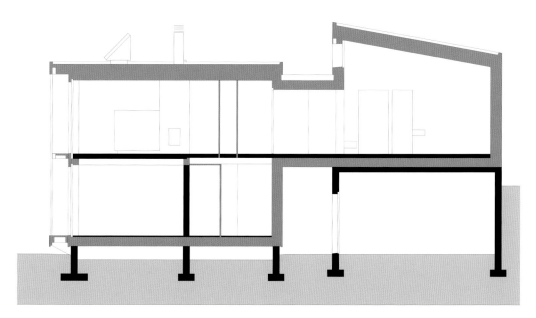

← | Section
↓ | Stove

Simone Giostra & Partners

↑ | **Entrance area** by night
→ | **Perspective** by night

GreenPix – Zero Energy Media Wall

Beijing

The façade of the entertainment center combines a color LED display measuring 2,200 square meters with a photovoltaic system integrated into a glass curtain wall. The building envelope becomes a self-sufficient organic system, harvesting solar energy by day and using it to illuminate the screen by night, mirroring the day's climatic cycle. The opaque box-like commercial building gains the ability of communicating with its urban environment through a new kind of digital transparency. Its "intelligent skin" interacts with the building interiors and the outer public spaces using embedded, custom-designed software, transforming the building façade into a responsive stage for entertainment and public engagement.

PROJECT FACTS

Address: Xicui Road, Beijing, China. **Lighting designer and façade engineer:** Arup. **Solar technology research and development:** Schüco International KG, Sunways AG. **Client:** Zhang Yongduo, Jingya Corporation. **Completion:** 2008. **Ecological aspects:** solar energy; photovoltaics laminated in meter-square low, medium, and high-transparency glass panels, absorbing solar energy during the day and generating light from the same power in the evening. **Certificates / standards:** zero energy building.

↑ | **Façade**
↓ | **LED construction**

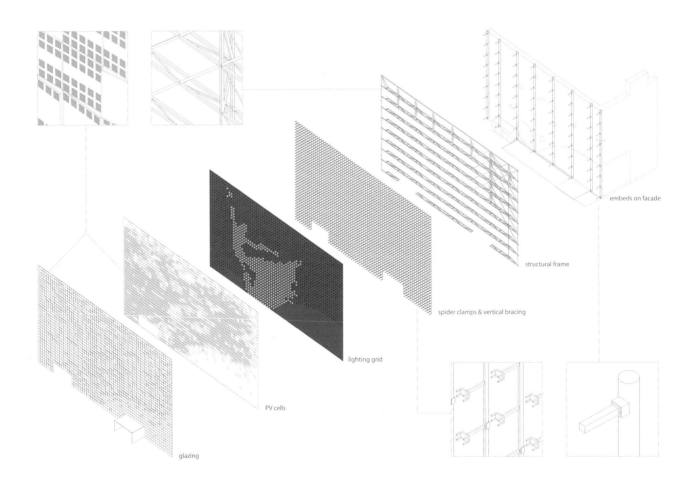

embeds on facade

structural frame

spider clamps & vertical bracing

lighting grid

PV cells

glazing

← | **LED detail**
↙ | **Façade,** detail
↓ | **Façade diagram**

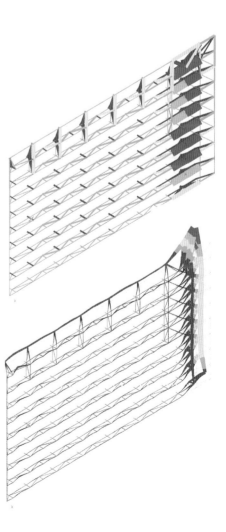

opus Architekten /
Prof. Anke Mensing,
Andreas Sedler

↑ | **Façade** by night
→ | **View** through the building

opusHouse
Darmstadt

The two-story Wilhelminian apartment building was bookended by taller neighbors and
an empty lot. The historic building received a floor addition which followed the measure-
ments and style of the existing architecture. The empty site, in contrast, was filled with
a modern three-story transparent extension, whose façade has proportions that reflect
those of the surroundings. Here, apartments and offices for opus Architekten have been
created. The addition of a story and an office is modeled on the passive house concept,
and the roof houses photovoltaic and solar thermal systems.

PROJECT FACTS

Address: Ploenniesstraße 14–16, 64289 Darmstadt, Germany. **Energy concept:** InPlan Ingenieurbüro für innovative Planung. **MEP engineer:** Binge + Berger Ingenieure, Jergus Ingenieurbüro für technische Gebäudeausrüstung. **Client:** Anke Mensing. **Completion:** 2007. **Ecological aspects:** solar energy; solar heat; heat pumps, recovery; rainwater reuse. **Certificates/standards:** low energy building (existing section)/passive energy building (new structure).

←← | **Elevated roof** (over added story)
↙↙ | **Living area** on added story
← | **Office,** new building
↓ | **Floor plans,** ground floor, first floor, second floor and elevated roof

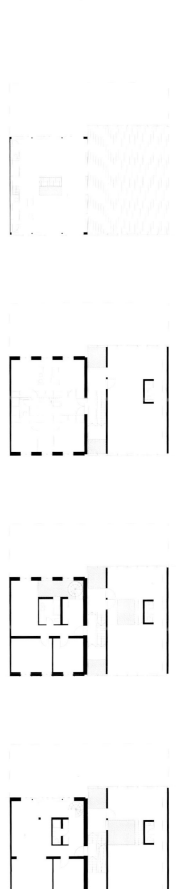

FAR frohn&rojas

↑ | **Exterior view** at night
→ | **Underneath the layers**

Wall House

Santiago de Chile

The basic concept of the building with separated wall layers combines aesthetic value with a sustainable approach. A series of specific climate zones are generated between the membranes, forming an energetic hierarchy. Gas-powered radiant heating is located inside the concrete core and the concrete ground floor slab. The slab radiates heat for the ground floor while the concrete core with integrated PEX-tubing radiates heat to the floor above. During the summer months, the circuit can be used as a passive cooling system with the help of a heat pump. The "milky shell", a translucent climate envelope, encompasses the interior space. The outer "soft skin" consists of two textile membranes.

PROJECT FACTS

Address: Avenida España 1750, Santiago de Chile, Chile. **Wood structure:** Ingewag, Mario Wagner. **Concrete structure:** Ernesto Villalón. **Bioclimatic project:** Central TechnoPlus/Vaillant, Nelson Quilaqueo, Cristian Aguirre. **Client:** Patricia Krause Senft. **Completion:** 2007. **Ecological aspects:** energy screen; heat pump. **Certificates/standards:** zero heating energy building.

↑ | **Interior view**
↙ | **Layers**
↓ | **Climate concept,** winter and summer
→ | **View from inside**

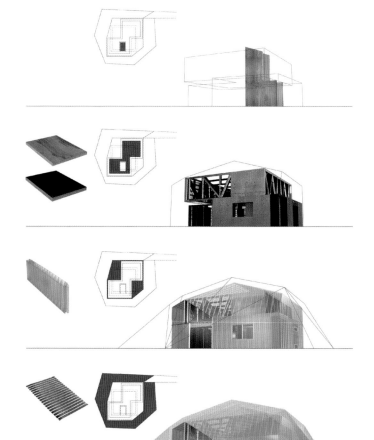

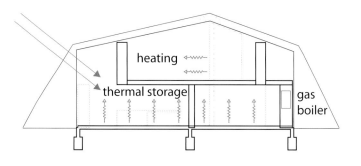

heating
thermal storage
gas boiler

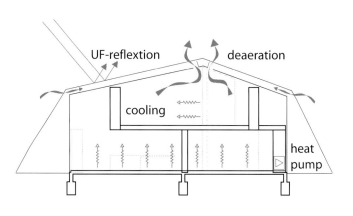

UF-reflextion   deaeration
cooling
heat pump

Studio Granda

↑ | **South-west view**
↗ | **Front view**
→ | **Cladding detail**

Hof

Hofðaströnd

The country residence has a remote and very special location, less than 100 kilometers from the Arctic Circle. It rises from the tufted site as a series of sheer cedar and concrete walls with displaced grass of the field reinstated on the roof. Raw or painted concrete was used for all innermost walls. Ceilings, doors and carpentry consist predominantly of oiled oak with steel details. The house is highly insulated and thermally stable due to massive concrete walls, stone floors and balanced fenestration. Geothermal water is used for floor heating, radiators and all domestic uses. Electricity consumption is minimized by design and sourced from hydroelectric and geothermal sources.

PROJECT FACTS

Address: Hof, 566 Höfðaströnd, Hofsós, Iceland. **MEP engineer:** Viðsjá. **Client:** Lilja Pálmadóttir and Baltasar Baltasarsson. **Completion:** 2007. **Ecological aspects:** geothermal, hydro energy; 100% renewable energy; recycled telegraph poles, stone from foundation excavation; transmission heat loss U=0.2 W/m²K (roof), U=0.4 W/m²K (walls); insulation glazing U ≤ 2 W/m²K; 270 m² covered with green.

↖ | Kitchen area
↑ | Parlor
← | Roof light detail

↖ | Bedroom corridor
↑ | Main bathroom
↓ | Sections

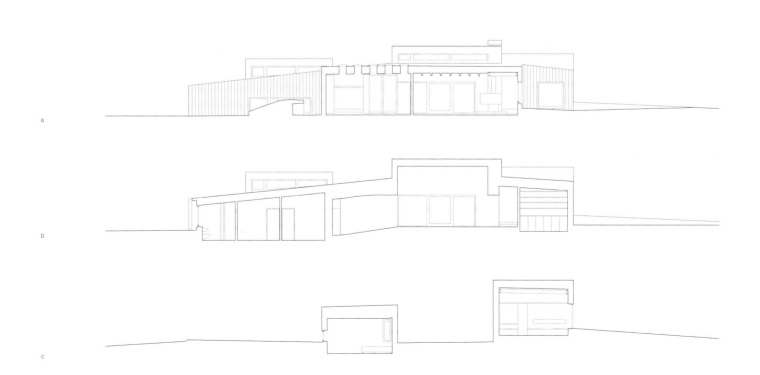

a

b

c

↑ | **Yoga on the roof**
→ | **The lounging hill**

Mini Rooftop
New York City

Based on BMW's Mini Cooper division's "Creative Use of Space" campaign, the no-energy outdoor event space is a temporary location fusing natural and artificial elements. An organic hill is suspended in an abstract architectural grid to create a jarring break with the typical landscape of the city. The roof flooring is made from Kay-Cel, which is also used for insulation of ice-skating-rings; here it helps to avoid heat-gain in the building. A grassy lounging hill with seating dimples, a performance stage and a panorama bar overlooking the Hudson River make the rooftop an ecological and social habitat within the urban grid.

PROJECT FACTS

Address: 465 10th Avenue, New York City, NY 10017, USA. **Planning partner:** AFORM Architecture, KREATIVEKONZEPTION, RADAR, GPJ. **Client:** BMW AG, MINI Brand. **Completion:** 2008. **Ecological aspects:** no energy outdoor event space; 85% of the material used is recyclable; water irrigation system to water the grassy hill, surface helps avoiding heat-gain in the building.

↖ | Tree over Manhattan
← | The rooftop and the skyline
↓ | Floor plan

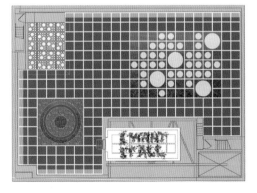

← | In the evening
↓ | Event

Medium

Kossmann.dejong,
Döll – Atelier voor Bouwkunst

↑ | **Entrance area,** cashpoint
↗ | **Checkroom**
→ | **Corridor**

Pop Stage WATT
Rotterdam

Organized as a city with rooms of different atmosphere along a central street, WATT intro-
duces experimental sustainable features such as a low-energy generating dance floor and
minimal wastebars. The larger relax-roof has a receptacle for rainwater, which conserves
more than 50,000 toilet flushes per year. The use of LED lighting instead of standard theater bulbs provides an 80 % reduction of electricity consumption. A sophisticated building
management system ensures efficient use of the climate system. A future large LED wall on
the main façade communicates the sustainable aspects of WATT with the environment and
the vegetated side wall will become a vertical continuation of the adjacent park.

PROJECT FACTS

Address: West-Kruiskade 26–28, 3014 AS Rotterdam, The Netherlands. **Client:** Vinc Batenburg, Brother-hood holding. **Completion:** 2008. **Ecological aspects:** sustainable dancefloor; 100% renewable energy; recycled wood, PVC; rainwater reuse; complete building automation; minimal waste bar; LED lighting; 270 m² covered with green. **Certificates/standards:** Sustainable Dance Club™.

↑ | **Dance floor**
← | **Entrance area**

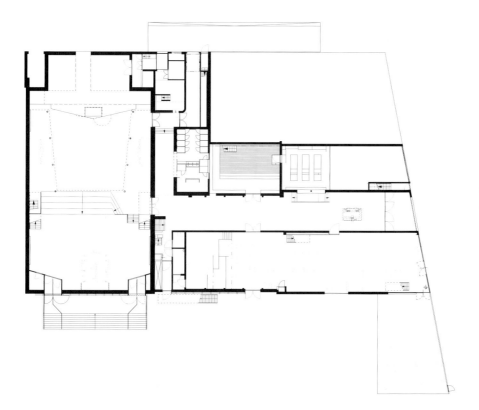

← | **Ground floor plan**
↓ | **Lounge area** and theater stage

The Kubala Washatko
Architects, Inc.

↑ | **Aerial view** of the courtyard
→ | **Aqueducts** made from recycled stone
masonry

Aldo Leopold Legacy Center
Baraboo

The new headquarter of the foundation remains true to the ecological, aesthetic, and scientific spirit of Aldo Leopold's Land Ethic. Aldo Leopold (1887–1948) was an ecologist, forester, and environmentalist, influential in the development of modern environmental ethics in America. Trees originally planted by Aldo Leopold have been used for the building. In October 2007 it received a LEED Platinum rating and became the highest-rated building evaluated under the USGBC rating system. It is the first building recognized by LEED as carbon neutral in operation. The 39-kilowatt solar photovoltaic array produces 61,000 kilowatt hours of electricity annually, 110% of what the building needs.

PROJECT FACTS

Address: E13701 Levee Road, Baraboo, WI 53913, USA. **MEP engineer:** Bob Eliopolous, The Matrix Group. **Client:** The Aldo Leopold Foundation. **Completion:** 2007. **Ecological aspects:** solar energy; solar heat; heat reservoir, exchanger, pumps, recovery; earth tube air ventilation system; transmission heat loss R-27 (walls), R-30 (roof); insulation glazing; ventilation engineering; rainwater collection. **Degree of sealing:** 69%. **Certificates / standards:** Energy-plus building, LEED Platinum; AIA COTE Top Ten Green Project.

↑ | **Administration wing**
↙ | **Bioclimatic building section diagram**

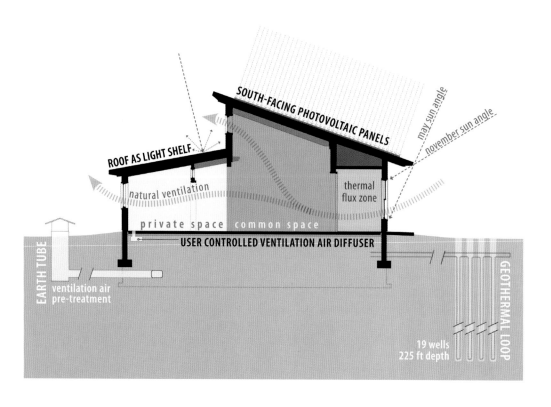

← | **Aerial view,** roofs with PV panels
↓ | **Ground floor plan**

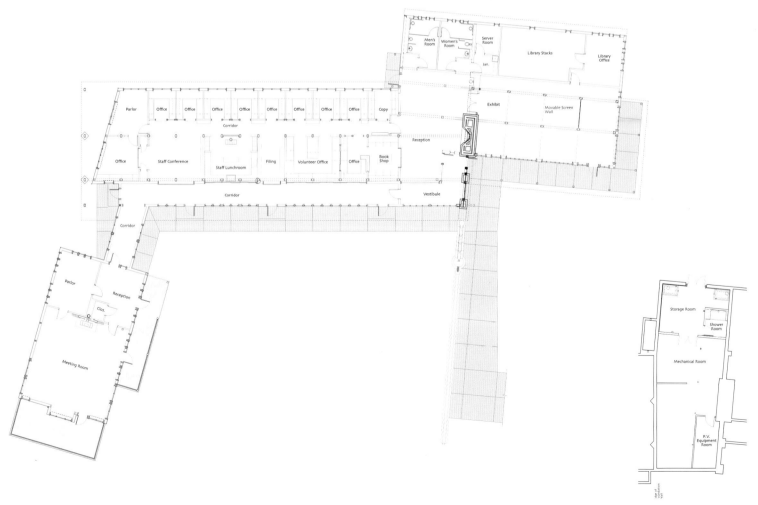

Ateliers Jean Nouvel

↑ | **Vegetal wall** covering the façade of the
Branly administrative building
→ | **Exterior view,** exhibition building

Musée du Quai Branly
Paris

The museum collects various exhibits stemming from non-European cultures which were
earlier dispersed among the city's various museums. The building is located in a generous garden, and the ground story remains open, allowing the garden sections to fuse
underneath the museum. The 18,000 square-meter garden takes up diverse vegetation as
its theme. A 12-meter-high, 200-meter-long glass wall shields the park from the busy Quai
Branly. The 800 square meters of the exterior and 150 square meters of the interior of the
green wall along the west perimeter along Quai Branly bring together 15,000 examples of
plants from Japan, China, the Americas and Central Europe.

PROJECT FACTS

Address: 55 Quai Branly, 198 rue de l'Université, 75007 Paris, France. **Lighting designer:** AIK – Yann Kersalé. **Vegetal wall:** Patrick Blanc. **Landscape architect:** Acanthe – Gilles Clément. **Client:** Etablissement public du Musée du Quai Branly. **Completion:** 2006. **Ecological aspects:** thermoactive building systems; insulation glazing; ventilation engineering; 800 m² covered with green.

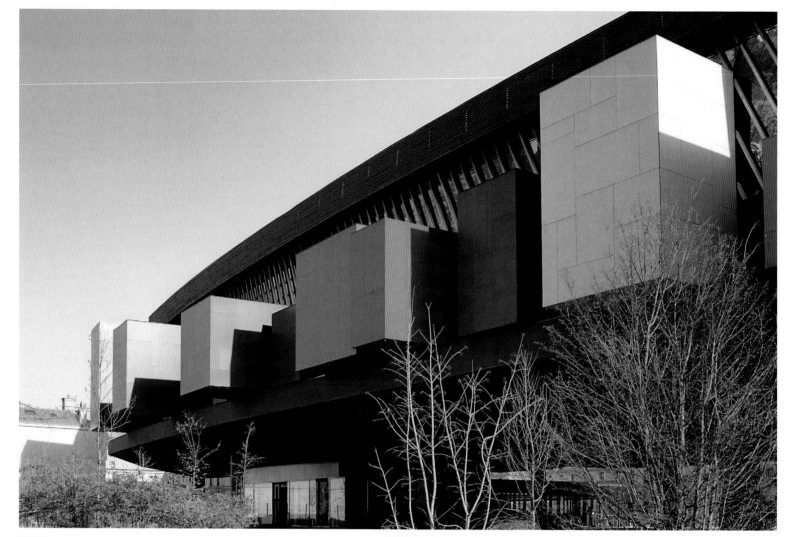

↑ | **Façade** with boxes
← | **University building**

← | **Glass palisade** on the banks of the Seine
↓ | **Sections**

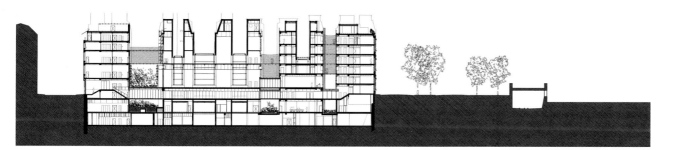

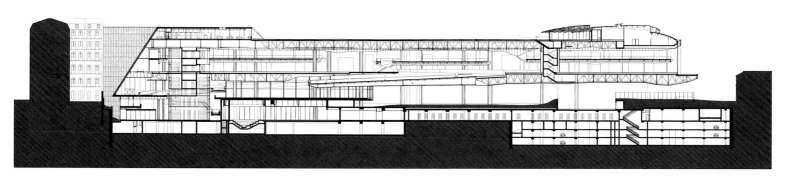

↑ | **Mezzanine**
→ | **Exterior view** on the north-east

Lavin-Bernick Center
for University Life

New Orleans

Balconies, canopies, shading systems, and courtyards create layered spaces which encourage the movement of people, light, and air in ways similar to vernacular buildings in New Orleans. Programs such as dining, conference facilities, an auditorium, offices, and a wide range of informal gathering/study spaces were located in relation to activity levels and needs for natural light and connections to the exterior. The hot and humid New Orleans climate is further tempered with strategies for expanding the comfort zone including programming for thermal zoning, and technically innovative systems for variable shading, moving air, and radiant cooling. The existing concrete structure was reused.

PROJECT FACTS

Address: 6823 St. Charles Avenue, New Orleans, LA 70118, USA. **Planning partners:** James Carpenter Design Associates and Transsolar Energietechnik GmbH. **Client:** Tulane University. **Completion:** 2007. **Ecological aspects:** daylight utilization, shading and passive cooling; heat recovery; reuse of existing concrete structure; complete building automation; ventilation engineering. **Certificates/standards:** low energy building, AIA COTE Top Ten Green Project 2008.

↑ | **View of entry at night**
← | **First floor plan**

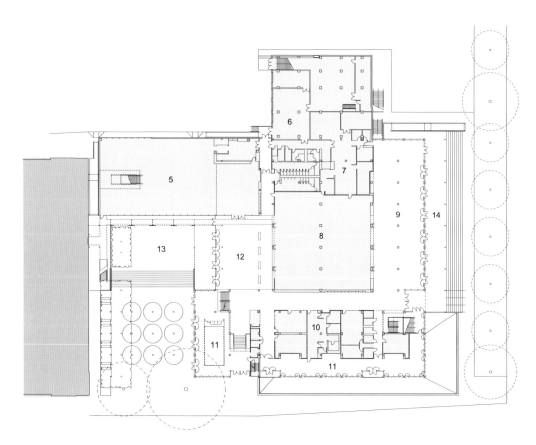

← | **Balcony** and shading canopy
↓ | **Commons space**

↑ | View from street
→ | View from archaeological garden

House near the Cathedral

Frankfurt/Main

Going along with the central idea of the general urban plan, the cathedral house creates scale through organization of its structural elements. The building is a contribution to the careful renewal of Frankfurt's historical city center, whose main objective is the preservation of architecturally significant parts of the customs office from the 1920s. Keeping down construction costs and the ecology of the building were also a high priority. The layout of the new structure was made using thermal simulation. Building infrastructure was planned while keeping investment and operation costs, as well as sustainability indicators in mind.

Address: Domplatz 3, 60311 Frankfurt /Main, Germany. **Planning partner:** Benjamin Jourdan, Felix Jourdan, Nicolai Steinhauser. **MEP engineer:** Ingenieurbüro Peter Berchtold. **Structural engineer:** S.A.N., Darmstadt. **Client:** Bistum Limburg, Bischöfliches Ordinariat. **Completion:** 2007. **Ecological aspects:** thermoactive building systems; regrowing wood, reuse of existing rooms; transmission heat loss U= 0.29 W/m²K (part B), Low-E glazing; complete building automation. **Certificates/standards:** EnEV 2004.

↑ | **Conference room**
↓ | **Longitudinal section,** showing heterogeneous functions

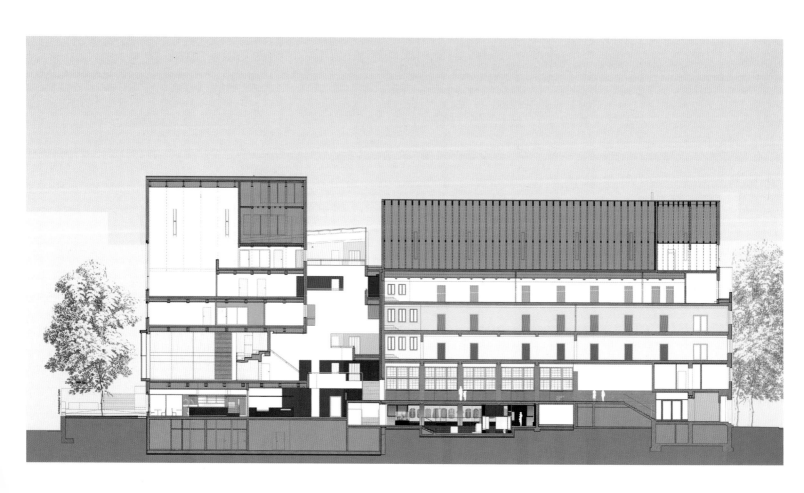

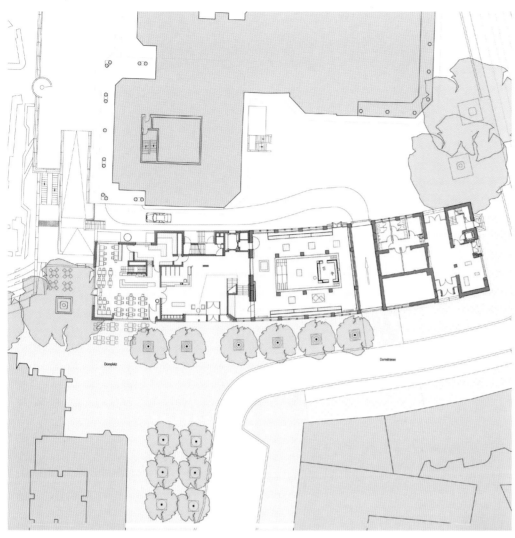

← | **Site** with ground floor plan
↓ | **Gable hall**

↑ | **View from Triftbach**
→ | **Thermal cupola** with outdoor basin

Spa / Thermal Baths
Bad Aibling

The concept for the spa is based on dome-shaped cabinets that house various attractions and uses. These are located below a spacious glazed hall, and partially protrude out from it. The climate regulation concept uses the spatial separation of the hall to create the optimal climate that corresponds to the specific demands within each dome and the hall, thereby reducing energy use. The relocation of the water surface to the domes in combination with air inlet in the hall and air draw-off in the domes results in a moist, warm climate in the domes and cooler temperatures in the hall. The glazed hall also facilitates solar preheating.

PROJECT FACTS

Address: Lindenstraße 32, 83043 Bad Aibling, Germany. **Climate concept:** Transsolar Energietechnik GmbH, Stuttgart. **MEP engineer:** IB Wach, Müller & Bleher. **Structural engineer:** Duwe Mühlhausen Ingenieurgesellschaft. **Light design:** IB Bamberger. **Client:** Stadtwerke Bad Aibling. **Completion:** 2007. **Ecological aspects:** thermal zoning to reduce energy consumption and ensure pleasant climatic conditions; heat recovery; optimized daylight exploitation; possible to switch from mechanical to natural ventilation.

←← | **Recreation cupola**
← | **Basin** with recreation level
↑ | **Sketch**
↓ | **Ground floor plan**

BVN Architecture /
Phil Page, Craig Burns,
Warwick Simmonds

↑ | **South façade,** perspective
→ | **North façade**

RAAF Richmond 36/37 Squadron Headquarters
Richmond

The Squadron Headquarters building provides workplace accommodation and shared support facilities for two squadrons in a secure, cost effective and environmentally advanced design. A high level of architectural amenity is achieved by its clear and flexible organization. Modular design and use of prefabricated elements minimized material consumption and enabled easy modification and deconstruction. Care was taken to extensively use recycled materials such as remilled timber for cladding, which reduced waste. Strategies such as rainwater collection and reticulation for toilet flushing and water-efficient appliances minimize the building's demand for mains water.

PROJECT FACTS

Address: Percival Street, Richmond 2755, NSW, Australia. **MEP engineer:** Rudds Consulting Engineers, Arup. **Client:** Department of Defence. **Completion:** 2006. **Ecological aspects:** minimized solar load, exposed thermal mass reduces cooling demand; recycled blackbutt timber cladding; regrowing timber, eco-labelled textiles; rainwater reuse; complete building automation; ventilation engineering. **Certificates/standards:** low energy building, 5 Star Green Star.

↑ | **Main workspace**
← | **East façade**

← | **Detail**, façade
↓ | **Ground floor plan**

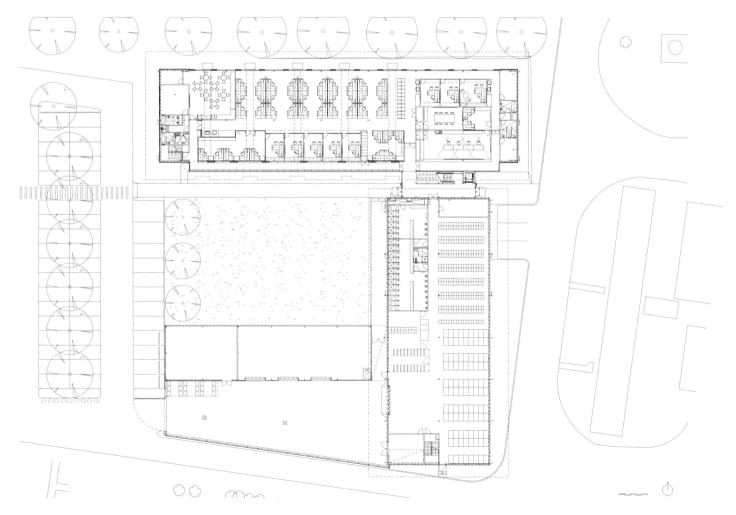

Alejandro Aravena

↑ | **Front elevation**

Siamese Towers

Santiago de Chile

The program for this glass tower saw the creation of 50,000 square meters to house computer workspaces and classrooms. The varying daylight requirements of classrooms and libraries, which need plenty of light to create an inviting atmosphere, and computer workspaces, which need shade to avoid screen reflection, were resolved with a compromise. A relatively hermetic bi-cephalous volume with controlled perforations to the outside is the result. The building consists of an internal fiber-cement structure with superior energetic attributes and an outer glass skin, which protects the building from weathering. The space between the skin and the inner building serves as a chimney, letting hot air exit the system at the top.

Address: Campus San joaquin Universidad Católica de Chile, Santiago de Chile, Chile. **Planning partner:** Ricardo Torrejón, Charles Murray, Alfonso Montero. **Collaborator:** Emilio De la Cerda. **MEP engineer:** Serinco Ltda. **Structural engineer:** Luis Soler y Asociados. **Client:** Pontificia Universidad Católica de Chile. **Completion:** 2005. **Ecological aspects:** insulation glazing; ventilation engineering. **Degree of sealing:** 15%.

↑ | Between façade skin and inner building volume
↓ | First floor plan

↑ | Exterior view
↓ | Ramp structure of untreated wood

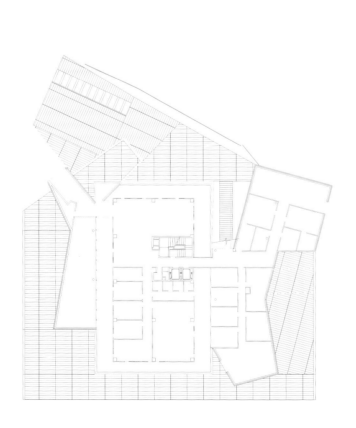

↑ | **Side elevation**
→ | **Entrance**

RömerMuseum

Archaeological Park Xanten

The museum building erected on the foundation of a former thermal baths vestibule compliments the protective excavation sheds built in the 1990s and allows the Roman bath complex to be explored by visitors. It mirrors the historical spatial proportions and rests the main load-bearing structure, a box-like meter-deep steel frame, on top of the historical walls. The exposition level, a delicate steel structure suspended from the frame, is designed as a self-developing surface extension in space. The vertical progression of the levels is experienced as a physically accessible time continuum and helps develop the exhibition as a historic voyage through the Roman epoch.

PROJECT FACTS

Address: Archäologischer Park Xanten, Siegfriedstraße 39, 46509 Xanten, Germany. **MEP engineer:** IGK-IGR Ingenieurgeschellschaft Kruck. **Artist:** Thomas Weii. **Client:** Landschaftsverband Rheinland. **Completion:** 2008. **Ecological aspects:** geothermal energy; 100% renewable energy; heat exchanger, pumps, recovery; 36 ground probes; recycled steel, glass, aluminum; façade elements, glass panel with core; rainwater reuse; sustainable engineering places steel framework on top of historical brickwork.

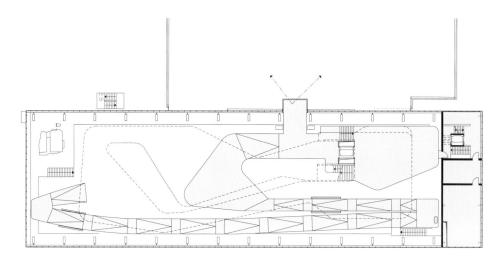

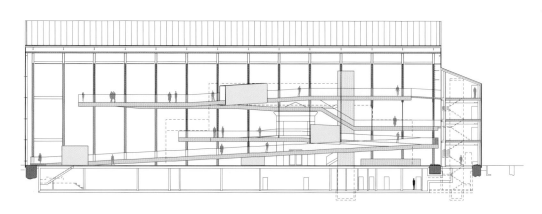

←← | **Interior view**
↖ | **Ground floor plan**
↙ | **Section**
↓ | **New façade** resting on historical brickwork

Despang Architekten

↑ | **Façade** with wood laths
→ | **Entrance area**

Postfossil Ecowoodbox Kindergarten

Hanover

The new kindergarten building for the first post-fossil generation is a sign of modernity in a quarter otherwise characterized by energy-intensive post-war architecture. It replaces an older building, which had a nearly identical ground plan, letting the existing soil sealing and building elements be reused for the new structure. Sunlight is utilized on the southern façade with the help of generous glazing while other sides are insulated and sheathed by thermally modified timber by Stora Enso, allowing the building act as a passive house. This also optically extends children's group rooms into the garden. Thanks to its natural materials, the building emanates a special peace and sensuality.

PROJECT FACTS
Address: Große Pranke 5, 30419 Hanover, Germany. **Client:** City of Hanover. **Completion:** 2007. **Eco-logical aspects:** solar energy; no sealing due to reuse of old situation. **Certificate/standards:** passive energy house.

↑ | View from courtyard
← | Façade detail

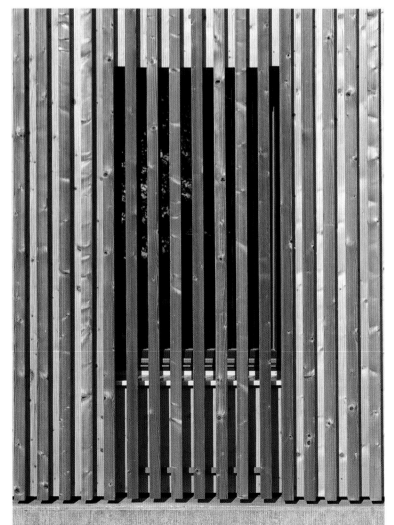

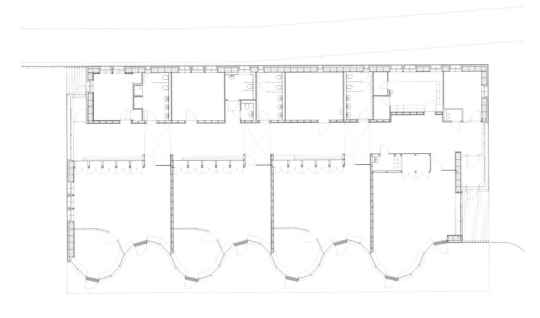

← | Ground floor plan
↓ | Corridor

Lapointe Architects

Fifth Town Artisan Cheese Factory

Picton

↑ | **Elevation** showing aging cave window and renaturalized site
→ | **Shaded sitting area** made from local reclaimed timber

This green facility produces fine artisan cheese and displays cheese production processes to the public. To minimize operational costs, energy from refrigeration and the pasteurization process is re-claimed and re-distributed throughout the building by way of a heat pump, heat exchanger, and geothermal ground loop. Furthermore, underground cheese aging caves utilize thermal mass while keeping the cheese on display. High humidity levels required by the production led to the use of structural blocks made from wood waste chips, stainless steel windows and doors, and epoxy coating to prevent corrosion. Production waste such as whey is handled responsibly through natural treatment within an artificial wetland.

PROJECT FACTS

Address: 4309 County Road #8 R. R. #4, Picton, ON, Canada. **MEP engineer:** Enermodal Engineering. **Client:** Fifth Town Artisan Cheese Co. **Completion:** 2008. **Ecological aspects:** solar, wind, geothermal energy; heat exchanger, pumps, recovery; transmission heat loss R-30 (walls), R-40 (roof), double and triple-glazed windows; rainwater reuse; automated lighting; 78 m² covered with green. **Certificates/standards:** low energy building, LEED Platinum (candidate).

↑ | **Entrance**
↓ | **Plan**

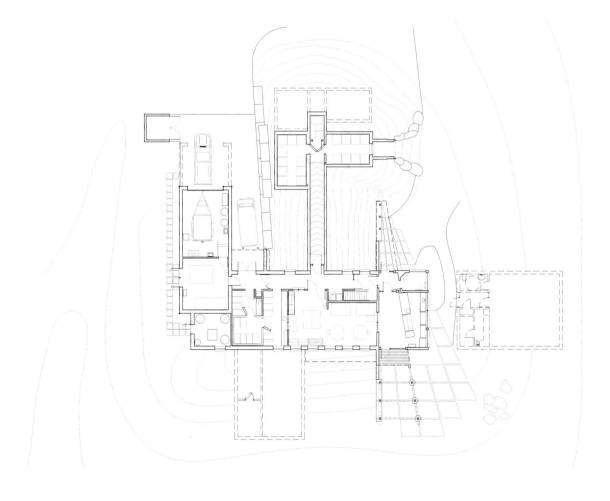

← | Sales counter
↙ | Aging caves

pfeifer roser kuhn
architekten

↑ | **Main entrance**
→ | **Façade detail**

Faller Pharma Service Center
Binzen

The building exemplifies less the spirit of the times than the contents of ecological construction. All exterior walls act as passive air collectors and consist of profile glazing positioned in front of the massive walls, separated from them by an empty space, but with no additional insulation. The building shape and zoning follow the principles of a Black Forest house with a central heat source. The massive concrete structure with a non-insulated baseplate regulates heat and enables climate control in production rooms using little energy. Recovery of machine heat exhaust in the winter months heats perimeter building sections.

PROJECT FACTS

Address: Meitner Ring 6, 79589 Binzen, Germany. **Cybernetics:** Delzer Kybernetik. **MEP engineer:** ratio energie GmbH. **Structural engineer:** Mohnke Bauingenieure. **Client:** August Faller KG. **Completion:** 2003. **Ecological aspects:** solar energy; use of process energy; solar heat; heat reservoir, recovery; thermoactive building systems; collector façade; regrowing wood; ventilation engineering; emissions reduction by 444 tons/year. **Degree of sealing:** 52 %.

↖ | **Office,** open space
← | **Kitchen corner**
↓ | **Energy concept**

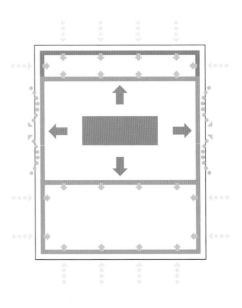

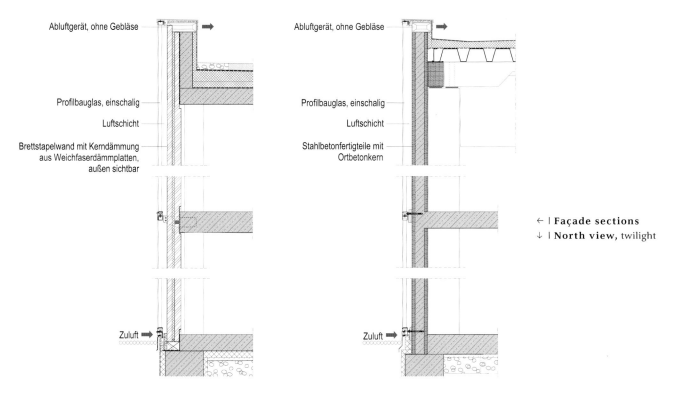

Abluftgerät, ohne Gebläse

Profilbauglas, einschalig

Luftschicht

Brettstapelwand mit Kerndämmung
aus Weichfaserdämmplatten,
außen sichtbar

Zuluft

Abluftgerät, ohne Gebläse

Profilbauglas, einschalig

Luftschicht

Stahlbetonfertigteile mit
Ortbetonkern

Zuluft

← | **Façade sections**
↓ | **North view,** twilight

ARCHTEAM,
RADAarchitects

↑ | **View from Orli Street**
→ | **View from Minorit's garden**

Theater Studio for JAMU University

Brno

The Theater Studio for JAMU University is situated in the historical center of Brno. The building's ground level offers a passage from the street to the garden, creating a leisure area that is suitable for meetings. The house is formed by two concrete bodies. One of them is low and matches the height of the neighboring older houses facing the street. The large receded body adjacent to the garden is covered with plush ivy. The basement contains a wine lounge. The foyer and a cafe are located downstairs, visually connected to the street by a glass façade. The building meets low-energy standards by using heat recovery systems and insulated glazings with heat mirrors.

PROJECT FACTS

Address: Orli Street 19, 602 00 Brno, Czech Republic. **Client:** University of Art. **Completion:** 2009.
Ecological aspects: thermal insulation using ivy-cladding and a green roof; 80% renewable energy;
heat pumps, recovery; thermoactive building systems; primary energy demand 12.1 kWh/m³a, transmission heat loss U=0.29 W/m²K; double glazing with heat mirror; complete building automation;
4,000 m² covered with greenery.

↑ | **View from Minorit's garden**
← | **Ground floor plan**

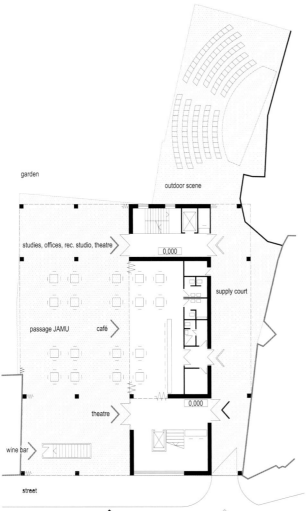

garden

outdoor scene

studies, offices, rec. studio, theatre

0,000

supply court

passage JAMU   café

0,000

theatre

wine bar

street

← | **Bird's-eye view** of the city block
↙ | **Street side view**

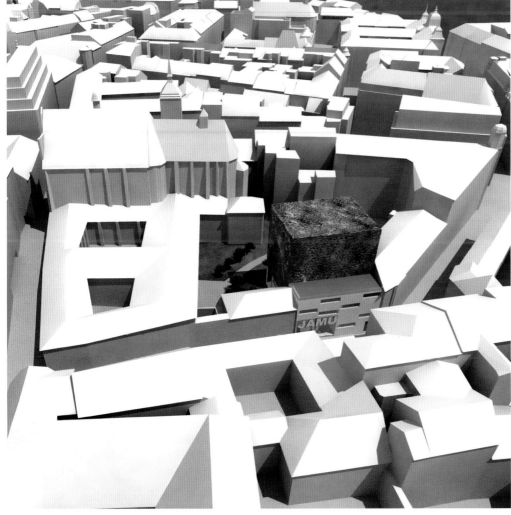

lutz architecte

↑ | **View from street**
↗ → | **Façade details**

Green Offices

Givisiez

This administrative building, which is the first in Switzerland to receive the Minergie-P-Eco label, is based on a minimalist approach to achieve the lowest possible energy consumption. Energy use optimization was made a priority during construction as well as in operation. The environmental impact of all building materials was analyzed, and ecological materials such as untreated wood, clay finish and recycled paper as thermal insulation were given priority. To reduce electricity and water use during operation, movement detectors, central light controls and a rainwater cistern were installed.

PROJECT FACTS

Address: 14, rue Jean Prouvé, 1762 Givisiez, Switzerland. **Structural engineer:** Vonlanthen Holzbau AG. **Completion:** 2007. **Ecological aspects:** solar, wind energy; 100% renewable energy; solar heat; pellet oven; recycled paper, regrowing wood; timer, motion sensor; rainwater reuse; complete building automation; ventilation engineering; arid WC. **Certificates/standards:** Minergie-P-Eco, Watt d'Or 2008.

↑ | **Office view** from staircase
← | **Staircase**

GREEN OFFICES

171

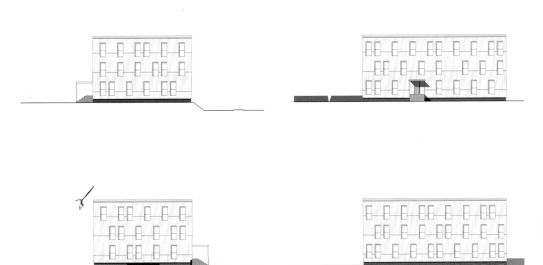

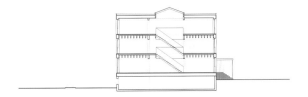

← | **Elevations** and section
↓ | **Interior view**

pfeifer. kuhn. architekten

↑ | **South façade** with air collector and energy garden
→ | **East façade**

Institute for Environmental Medicine and Hospital Hygiene
Freiburg

The goal of the research project was to develop a laboratory building which could lower primary energy consumption by up to 70% in comparison to conventional laboratories. The building is structured using various layers: labs on the northern side with outlying supply shafts, a central distribution zone with stairs and elevators and the open administrative zone with three energy gardens in the south, which improve the building's microclimate with greenery, ventilation and irrigation. The building's warming and cooling takes place via thermal air circulation with solar energy gain and thermal recovery and activation of massive building components using geothermal energy.

PROJECT FACTS

Address: Breisacher Straße 115b, 79110 Freiburg, Germany. **Architects:** until 30.06.2005 pfeifer roser kuhn architekten. **Cybernetics:** Delzer Kybernetik. **MEP engineer:** Kuder, Fein. **Structural engineer:** Mohnke Bauingenieure. **Client:** Federal State of Baden-Württemberg. **Completion:** 2006. **Ecological aspects:** solar, geothermal energy; solar heat; heat exchanger, pumps, recovery; thermoactive building systems; primary energy demand 46.3 kWh/m²a; rainwater reuse; complete building automation; ventilation engineering.

↑ | Corridor
↓ | Ground floor plan

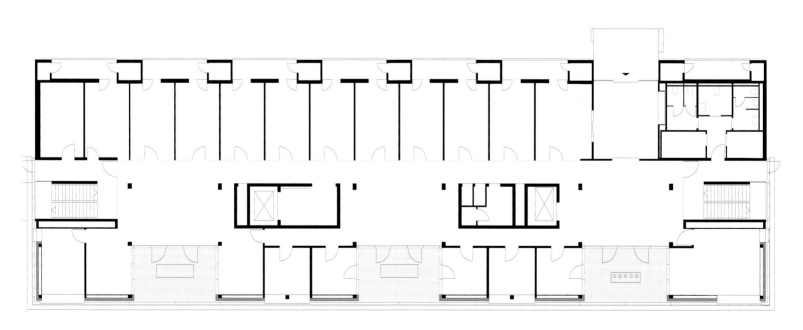

← | **Energy garden** with artwork by Wolfgang
Winter and Bertold Hörbelt
↓ | **Longitudinal section**

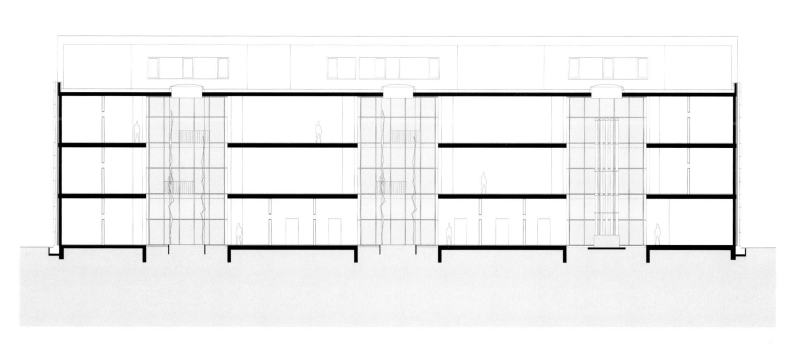

↑ | **Concept drawing**

Residence Antilia

Mumbai

Located on a Cumballa Hill overlooking the Arabian Sea and the city of Mumbai, the concept for this private residence produced a multi-tiered, landscaped structure. The entire building is conceived as a garden in the sky, freeing landscape from its normal earthbound confinement. The residence's seven levels are supported by a stratified structural spine reinforced with a series of steel cables that include five "floating" floor planes and a variety of interim garden tiers, terraces, viewing platforms, and recreational facilities. Generous daylight penetration enabled a reduction of energy consumption for artificial lighting. A seasonal monsoon water retention system runs from top to bottom as meandering fine water filtration channels and waterfalls.

PROJECT FACTS

Address: Cumballa Hill, Mumbai, India. **MEP engineer:** Jaros Baum and Bolles. **Structural engineer:** Weidlinger Associates Inc. **Artist:** Sara Stracey. **Landscape architect:** Matthews Nielsen Landscape Architecture. **Client:** Reliance Industries Limited. **Ecological aspects:** solar, wind, geothermal energy; solar heat; heat reservoir, exchanger; thermoactive building systems; rainwater reuse; complete building automation; ventilation engineering. **Degree of sealing:** 70%. **Certificates/standards:** LEED Gold (candidate).

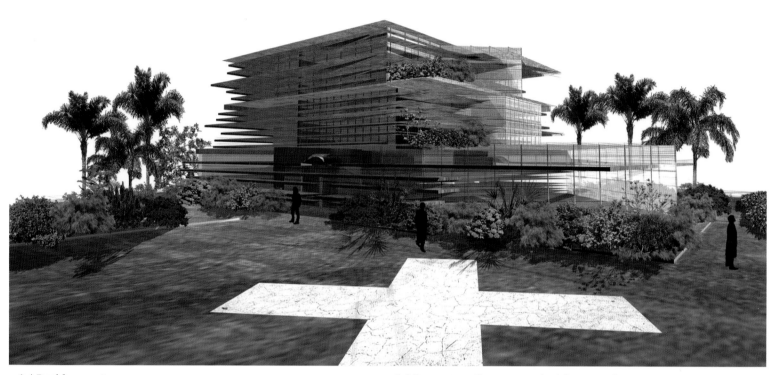

↑ | **Residence at apex**
↓ | **Conceptual sketch**

↓ | **Concept,** podium, open and semi-open garden

↑ | **Exterior view**
→ | **Side elevation**

Limerick County Council Headquarters

Limerick

The principal objective of the Limerick County Council Headquarters was to create a low energy building and to provide an environment that helped to reach the goals of "Better Local Government – Programme for Change" including the effective delivery of a wider range of public services, accessibility and accountability. This office building is naturally ventilated with a bespoke structural timber brise-soleil, combining both environmental control and structural stability to the southwest façade. The cross ventilation of the office spaces is driven by the thermal buoyancy of the atrium behind. The exposed concrete frame of the office spaces acts as a thermal sink to keep constant temperatures.

PROJECT FACTS

Address: Limerick County Council, County Hall, Dooradoyle, Co. Limerick, Ireland. **MEP engineer:** Buro Happold. **Client:** Limerick County Council. **Completion:** 2003. **Ecological aspects:** wind energy; 61% improvement in energy use; 0.8 m/s airflow for ventilation; natural ventilation. **Certificates/ standards:** Sustainable Energy Ireland, RIBA Sustainablility Award, RIBA Award, Mies van der Rohe Award (candidate), OPUS Award.

↑ | **Interior view**
↓ | **Ground floor plan**

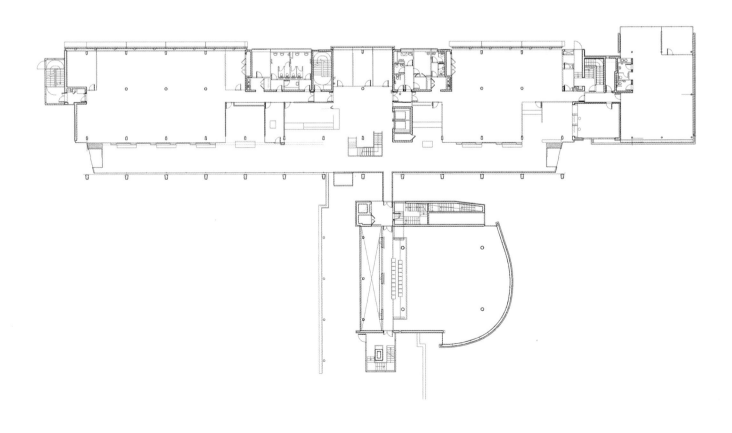

← | **Façade element** with a structural timber brise-soleil
↓ | **Diagram,** lighting and ventilation

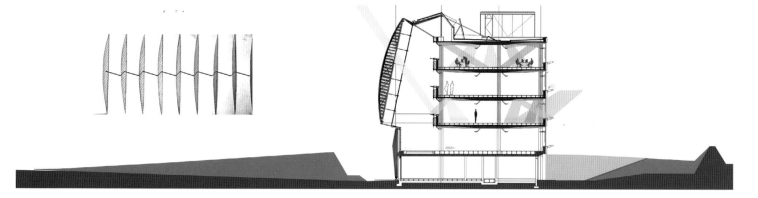

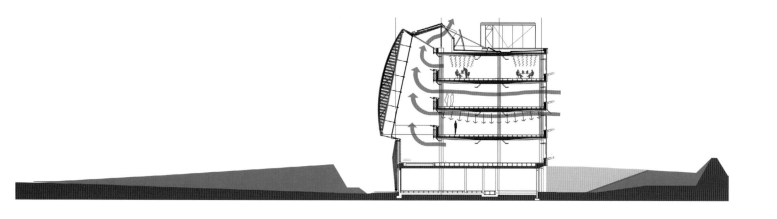

Riepl Riepl Architekten

↑ | **Tower building**
→ | **View from train station**

Train Station City

Wels

The tower forms a highly visible sign marking Wels's new urban center which strives to become Europe's energy capital. With a diversified program, Train Station City clearly frames the square and formulates the paths between various public institutions like the college, high school and hospital. In spite of the clear individual accents, the ensemble as a whole appears delicate and light. Tension comes about through the tug and pull of horizontal and vertical elements. Modern thin, semi-transparent photovoltaic collectors serve as replacements for typical double-glass windows and create shade.

PROJECT FACTS

Address: Bahnhofplatz 2–4, 4600 Wels, Austria. **MEP engineer:** TB Ökoenergie Greif. **Structural engineer:** DI Raffelsberger. **Client:** Consulting Company. **Completion:** 2006. **Ecological aspects:** solar energy.

↑ | **Atrium**
↓ | **Section**

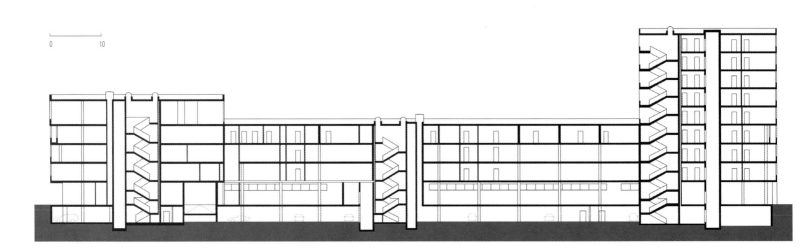

0   10

← | **Photovoltaic system** on the glass roof
↓ | **Ground floor plan**

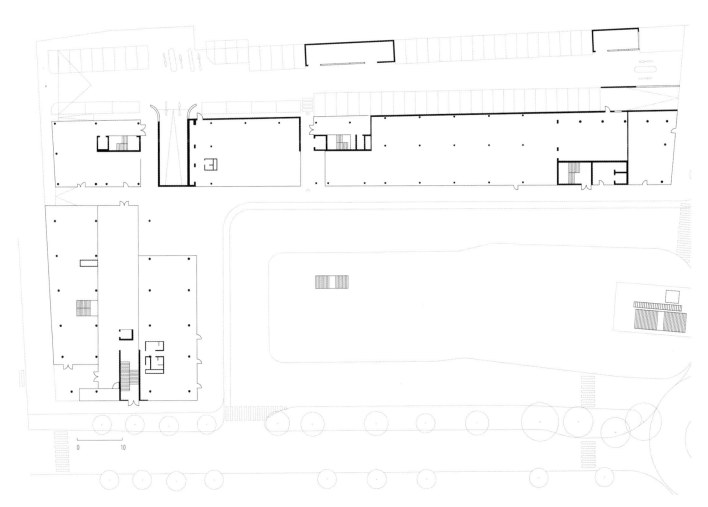

0   10

Antoine Predock

↑ | **Exterior view** at night
↓ | **West entry** with projection wall above

University of New Mexico School of Architecture & Planning

Albuquerque

The new library for the School of Architecture and Planning at the University of New Mexico is driven by the necessity of making a building that inspires and teaches students about the potential of architecture while creating a timeless relationship of building and environment in both the design concept as well as in a sustainable sense. Believing that a student can be engaged and actively learn from the intrinsic qualities of the spaces in which they work, the project accomplishes this by revealing infrastructure and environmental systems such as the cooling tower/solar engine loop and by demonstrating how plan and section are connected linking light, spatial flows and structure.

Address: 2401 Central Avenue, Albuquerque, NM 87131, USA. **Planning partner:** Jon Anderson Architect. **Client:** University of New Mexico School of Architecture & Planning. **Completion:** 2008. **Ecological aspects:** daylight harvesting, solar heat; heat reservoir, recovery; recycled steel, homasote; high performance glazing: Low-E solarban 60, fritted glass; motion sensors; rainwater reuse; ventilation engineering; waterless urinals, automatic electronic valves; 47.35 m^2 covered with greenery.

↑ | **Corner gallery** with clerestory windows
← | **Sketch**

← | Upper mezzanine studios
↙ | Vertical circulation

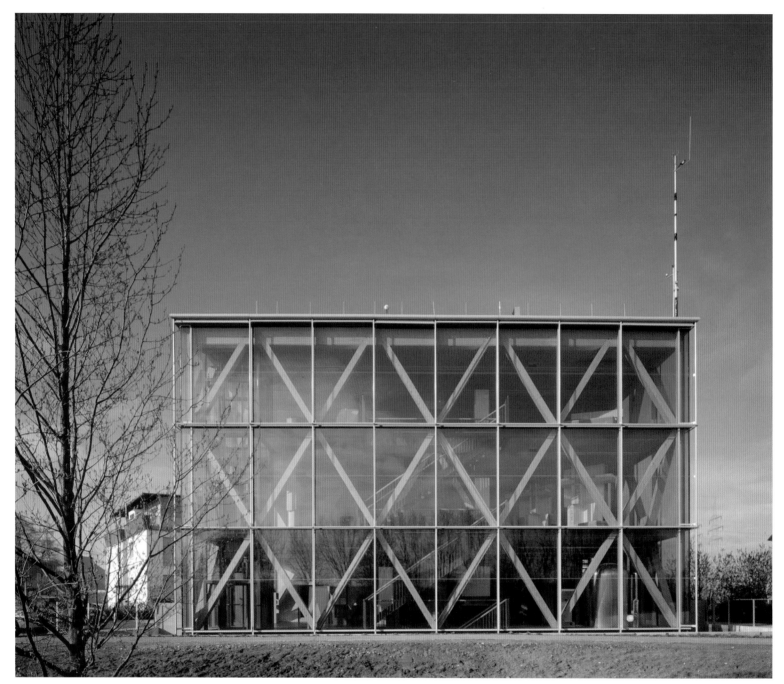

↑ | **Front elevation**
→ | **Perspective**

Paul-Schnitker-Haus
Münster

The Münster Trade Chamber has created a very unique demonstration and information center for craftsmen, engineers, architects and contractors with its new center for energy efficient and ecological construction. Already in its realization phase, the goal was set to steer the attention of project participants towards the buildings itself as well as ecological building materials. Energy consumption and construction behavior of the building were gathered and explained using measuring and presentation systems. In addition to the information and consultation forum, the buildings will house additional instruction and seminar rooms, offices and apartments for the chamber's guests.

PROJECT FACTS
Address: Franz-Meis-Straße 1–2, 48163 Münster, Germany. **Planning partner:** Fraunhofer Institut, Dr. Löfflad, Dr. Mohrhenne. **MEP engineer:** Ing. Ganter u. Wiemeler. **Client:** Handwerkskammer Münster. **Completion:** 2004. **Ecological aspects:** solar, geothermal energy; solar heat; heat reservoir, exchanger, pumps, recovery; thermoactive building systems; concrete activation; rainwater reuse; complete building automation; ventilation engineering. **Certificates/standards:** low/passive energy building.

↑ | **Interior view**
↙ | **Ground floor plan**

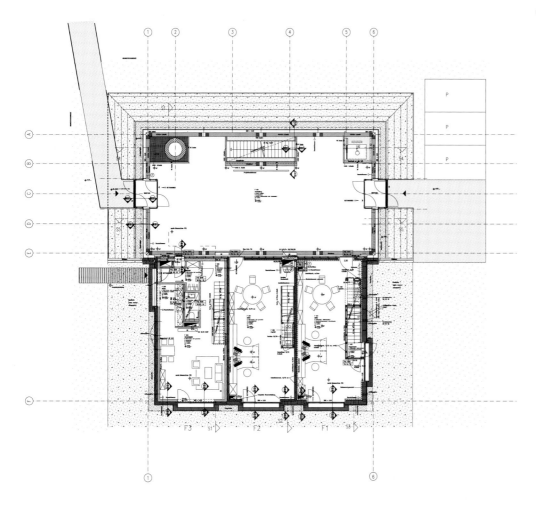

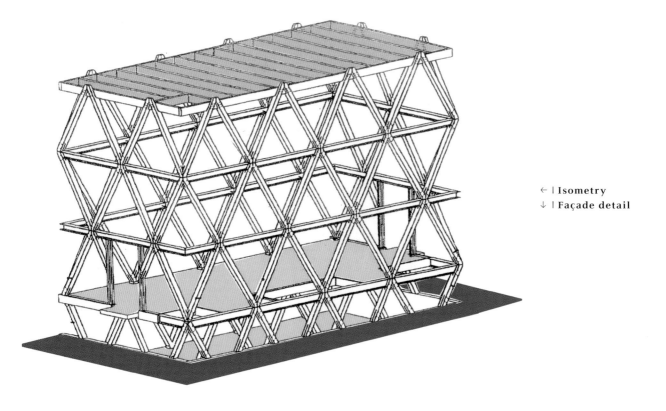

← | Isometry
↓ | Façade detail

Philippe Samyn and Partners
architects & engineers

↑ | **Glass façade**
→ | **The façade** consists of greenery extending to
the roof

Milly Film
Bruxelles

This mixed use structure creates production, work and residential space. The green façade is composed of a selection of exotic plants and extends to cover the roof. Various structural, insulation and water-tightness properties of the envelope had to be resolved in order to connect necessary support, irrigation and fertilization systems for the plants. The façade greenery was set into a support attached to rigid PVC panels. The green walls help to reduce energy consumption in response to thermal conditions. They provide exterior insulation, preventing heat discharge from within, and work as a natural cooling system.

PROJECT FACTS

Address: Bruxelles, Belgium. **Botanical artist:** Patrick Blanc. **Client:** Milly Films. **Completion:** 2007. **Ecological aspects:** thermoactive building systems; insulation glazing; rainwater reuse; ventilation engineering; 600 m² covered with greenery.

↑ | **Interior view**
↓ | **Section**

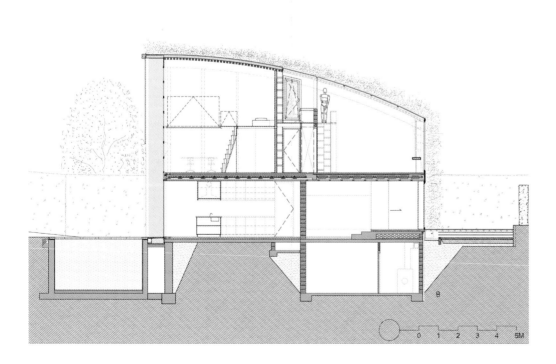

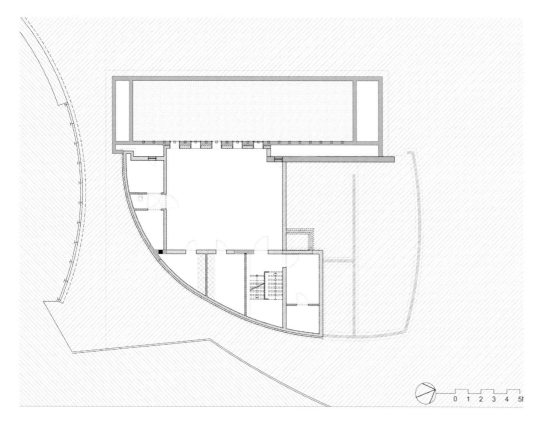

← | **Ground floor plan**
↓ | **Interior view** with roof structure

FXFOWLE Architects /
Guy Geier

↑ | **Conference rooms** and common area
→ | **Individual office**

National Audubon Society
New York

In the new Audubon headquarters, an elaborate design concept resulting in comfortable and friendly work spaces is combined with a range of sustainable strategies. All aspects of the National Audubon Society were considered, starting with a location that is close to subway and bus lines, allowing employees to take advantage of public transport, followed by a number of systems helping to reduce energy consumption of the building, and ending with the careful choice of recycled construction materials. An underflow air distribution system utilizing the natural buoyancy of air was integrated to heat the rooms. Large windows and an open office plan allow daylight penetration for the entire floor.

PROJECT FACTS

Address: 225 Varick Street, New York, NY 10014, USA. **MEP engineer:** WSP Flack + Kurtz. **Client:** National Audubon Society. **Ecological aspects:** energy efficient systems focused on conservation, energy star appliances; complete building automation with sensors and controls; under-floor air distribution system; high indoor environmental quality, low emission materials; alternative transportation; construction waste management plan. **Certificates / standards:** LEED Platinum – Commercial Interiors.

↑ | **Open office space**
← | **Reception** and lobby

← | **Hallway**, exposed wood
↓ | **Insight story**

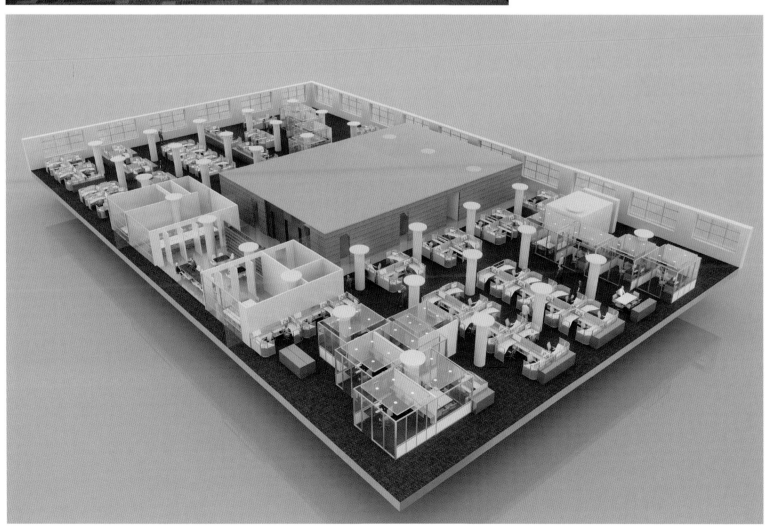

Michael Tribus Architecture

↑ | **View from main street**

Ex-Post
Bolzano

The former post office from 1954 has been modified to result in a modern office building for governmental agencies and constitutes the first public passive energy house in Italy, with a computed consumption of one liter of heating oil per square meter. Due to the high energy savings, all operating costs for the office building were reduced by approximately 90%. Insulated with a highly efficient building shell consisting of a polystyrene brick work and triple-pane glazing, it was possible to forgo a traditional heating system altogether. A ventilation unit with a heat recovery function is used for heating and cooling the offices, allowing individual thermal control for each room.

PROJECT FACTS

Address: Via Renon 4, 39100 Bolzano, Italy. **Ventilation engineering:** Menerga. **Client:** Autonomous Province of Bolzano. **Completion:** 2007. **Ecological aspects:** solar energy; heat recovery 90%, annual heat requirement: 7 kWh/m²a according to PHPP; walls with 35 cm EPS insulation; airtightness n50=0.6/h; insulation glazing U=0.6 W/m²K, g=54%; ventilation engineering. **Certificates/standards:** passive energy building, Klimahaus gold.

↑ | **Elevation,** back façade and photovoltaic plant
↓ | **Pipeline plan**

↓ | **Ventilation system** integrated in the door

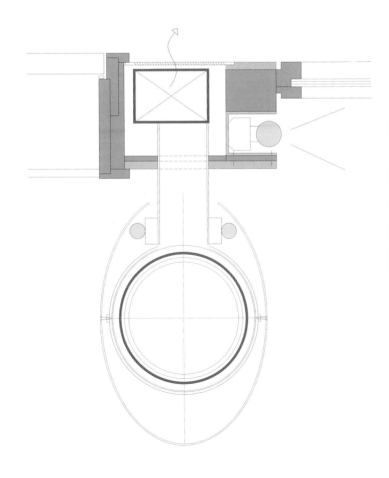

H Arquitectes /
David Lorente, Josep Ricart,
Xavier Ros, Roger Tudó

↑ | **Exterior view**
↗ | **Façade and forecourt**
→ | **Side elevation**

Gym 704
Barcelona

A simple prismatic volume, deformed only by the slope of the deck has been attached in parallel to the access ramp so as to avoid casting a shadow on the track, allowing an alternate use when the school is closed. The porch becomes the theme for the composition, providing access to locker rooms and the gym while connecting them to the level of the track sport area. The formalization of the building is achieved using constructive logic, which was part of the initial intention to build using microlaminated wood. The outer coating is made with polycarbonate panels, which contribute to energy savings on the southern façade and bring light to the north façade.

PROJECT FACTS

Address: Calle/Josep Mª de Segarra s/n, 08210 Barberà del Vallès, Barcelona, Spain. **Planning partner:** Anna Bullich, Blai Cabrero. **Cybernetics:** Iñaki de Mendiguchia. **Client:** Council of Barberà del Vallès. **Completion:** 2008. **Ecological aspects:** solar energy; solar heat; heat pumps, insulated by a trombe wall in the south façade; regrowing laminated wood panels, cork; transmission heat loss U=0.46 w/m²K; insulation glazing U=2.00 w/m²k. **Degree of sealing:** 24%.

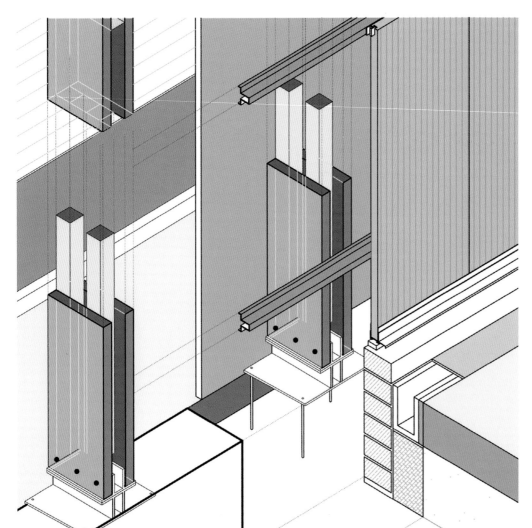

← | Façade construction
↓ | Interior view
→ | Perspective
↘ | Corner

Halle 58 Architekten

↑ | **South-west elevation,** blinds open
↗ | **South-west elevation,** blinds closed
→ | **South-east elevation**

Multifamily House
Liebefeld

On the space formerly occupied by seven old car sheds, the first Minergie-P-Eco multi-family home in Switzerland was built within the space of one year. The volume of the new building is organized according to the existing neighborhood structures, while its interiors offer a contemporary and future-oriented quality of life. The ship form of the wooden house's footprint is defined by the shape of the plot. The building was able to fulfill Minergie-P-Eco standard thanks to minimal thermal bridges, large windows to the southwest (passive use of the sun energy), sufficient thermal mass, good daylight utilization and consistent use of ecological building materials.

Address: Gebhartstrasse 15, 3097 Liebefeld, Switzerland. **Planning partner:** Peter Schürch, Fabian Schwarz. **MEP engineer:** Gartenmann Engineering AG. **Client:** community association. **Completion:** 2006. **Ecological aspects:** solar, wood pellets energy; 100% renewable energy; solar heat; heat reservoir; recycled concrete; energy consumption 56.3 kWh/m²; glass air conditioning skin triple glazing U=0.5 W/m²K; ventilation engineering. **Degree of sealing:** 21%. **Certificates/standards:** passive energy building; Minergie-P-Eco.

↑ | **Roof,** terrace and solar panels
↓ | **Cross section**

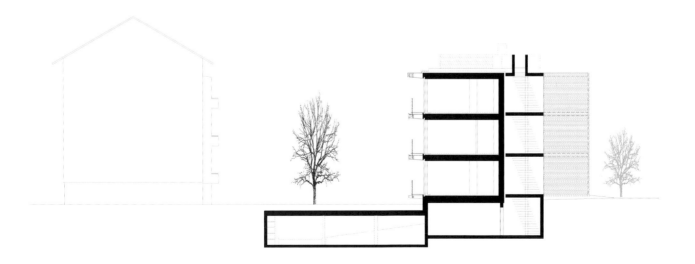

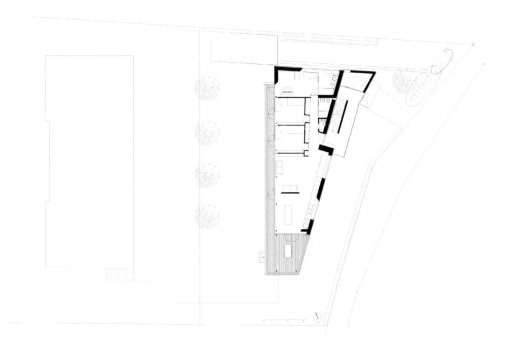

← | **Site plan** with ground floor
↓ | **Kitchen,** second level

Croxton Collaborative
Architects

↑ | **Entrance area**

Willingboro Master Plan and Public Library

Willingboro

Willingboro, NJ, one of the three original Levittowns in America, was suffering from dete-
rioration and economic loss that characterized the nation's 'First Ring' suburbs in the mid
1990's. Through a community-driven initiative, a sustainable master plan has transformed
Willingboro Plaza, a bankrupt, auto-centric, suburban, single-use project into a multi-pur-
pose, diverse, secure and community-focused town center anchored by the Willingboro
Public Library. The building is especially environment-friendly thanks to its 100% reuse
of the existing structural steel, as this structural material requires the most energy.

PROJECT FACTS

Address: 220 Willingboro Parkway, Willingboro, NJ 08046, USA. **Client:** Willingboro Township.
Completion: 2004. **Ecological aspects:** 57% reduction in peak electrical demand, 44% reduction
in carbon dioxide emissions; reuse of existing structural steel. **Certificates/standards:** AIA COTE
Top Ten Green Project 2007, Greater Philadelphia Sustainability Awards 2008.

↑ | **Interior view**
↓ | **Building section** and dappled light skylight

↑ | **Interior view**
↓ | **Interior view**, skylights

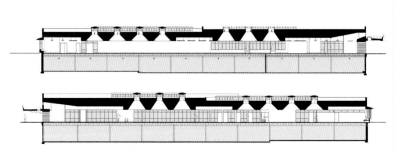

Mario Cucinella Architects

↑ | Side elevation
→ | View at night

Sino-Italian Eco Efficient Building

Bejing

The joint venture of Italian and Chinese governments houses the Sino-Italian education, training and research center for environmental protection and energy archiservation. It is designed as a showcase for the potential of CO_2 emissions reduction in China. The design integrates passive and active strategies to control the external environment in order to optimize internal environmental conditions. It is closed and well insulated on the northern side oriented to cold winter winds, and open and transparent towards the south. Offices and laboratories on the upper floors have terraced gardens shaded by photovoltaic panels that produce energy for the building.

PROJECT FACTS

Address: Tsinghua University, Bejing, China. **Structural engineer:** Favero & Milan Ingegneria. **MEP engineer:** Merloni Termosanitari Group, Fabriano. **Glass façade engineer:** Permasteelisa Spa, Vittorio Veneto. **Client:** Italian Ministry for Environment and Territory, Ministry of Science and Technology of the People's Republic of China. **Completion:** 2006. **Ecological aspects:** solar energy; trigenerator system; rainwater reuse. **Certificates/standards:** low energy building.

↑ | **Courtyard**
↙↓ | **Diagrams**, climate and ventilation

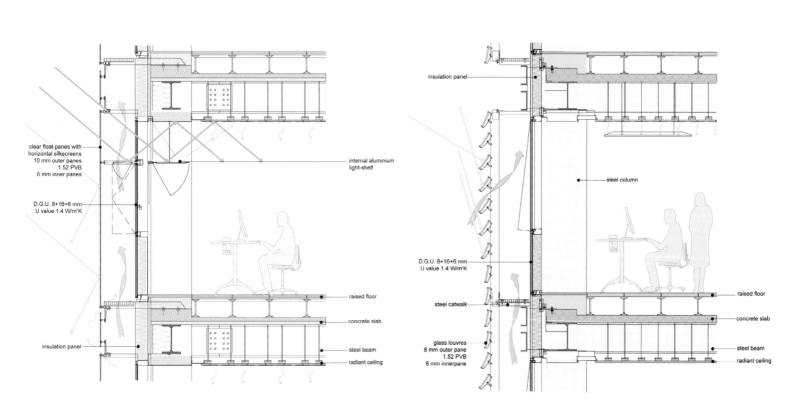

clear float panes with
horizontal silkscreens
10 mm outer panes
1.52 PVB
6 mm inner panes

D.G.U. 8+16+6 mm
U value 1.4 W/m²K

insulation panel

internal aluminium
light-shelf

raised floor

concrete slab

steel beam

radiant ceiling

insulation panel

steel column

D.G.U. 8+16+6 mm
U value 1.4 W/m²K

steel catwalk

glass louvres
8 mm outer pane
1.52 PVB
6 mm innerpane

raised floor

concrete slab

steel beam

radiant ceiling

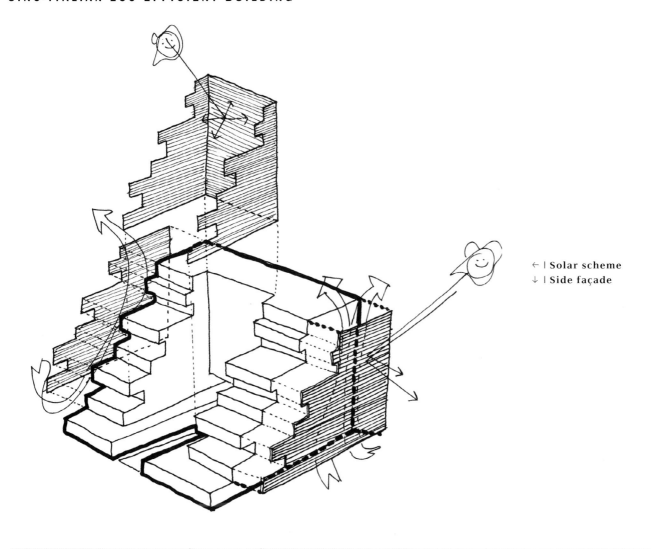

← | Solar scheme
↓ | Side façade

↑ | **North elevation,** overhang provides a
shaded outdoor reading space
→ | **The roof harvests and stores rain in an
adjacent lake for later use**

Cesar Chavez Branch Library
Phoenix

Located adjacent to an existing lake in a public park, the library is designed to serve a
projected flow of 40,000 visitors per month in one of the fastest growing areas of Phoenix, the Village of Laveen. The building is incised into an existing earth mound, quietly
integrating itself into the parkscape. Supplemented with soil excavated from the site this
mound acts as an insulating thermal mass, reducing strain placed on the mechanical system, and providing sound insulation. Sheltering roof planes shade the glass, and slope
towards a central roof channel, directing rain to the lake where it is stored and reused for
irrigation.

PROJECT FACTS

Address: 3635 W. Baseline Rd., Phoenix, AZ 85339, USA. **MEP engineer:** Energy Systems Design. **Client:** City of Phoenix. **Completion:** 2007. **Ecological aspects:** high efficiency heat pumps; recycled concrete, wood and steel; insulated double pane Low-E glazing; earth berming insulation; rainwater reuse. **Certificates/standards:** AIA COTE National Top Ten Green Building, LEED Silver (candidate).

↑ | **Earth berms** providing thermal mass, minimizing heating and cooling energy use
← | **Ground floor plan**
↓ | **Cross section**
→ | **Circulation space** in stacks widened for seating areas close to the books

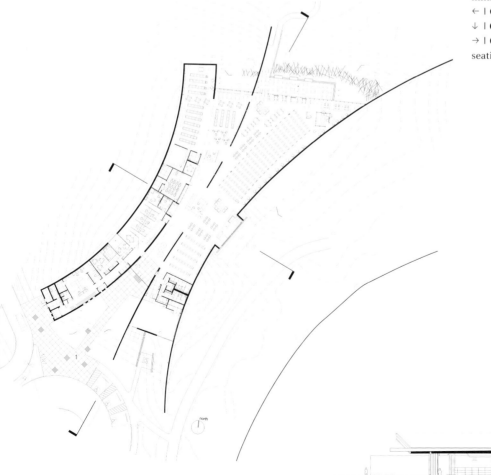

Pauat Architekten

↑ | **Side elevation**
↗ | **Front elevation** with entrance
→ | **Entrance area** with forecourt

School Rehabilitation
Schwanenstadt

The brief for rehabilitation of the school building as a demonstration on how passive house standards can be reached included the demand to raise the quality of use by improving air, daylight and climate control quality in the spaces. In addition, energy consumption during construction and operation had to be kept to a minimum. The school building was made more compact and covered by an ecologically top-grade envelope in order to improve the building's insulation properties. Interior areas were opened in order to optimize daylight use with skylights, and decentralized, energy-efficient space ventilation systems were integrated.

PROJECT FACTS

Address: Mühlfeldstraße 1, 4690 Schwanenstadt, Austria. **Structural engineer:** DI Bieregger, Obermayr Holzkonstruktionen GesmbH. **Completion:** 2007. **Ecological aspects:** redevelopment with passive house-qualified and ecologically sound envelope; innovative thermal rehabilitation of the floor slab using vacuum insulation panels with minimum floor rise height. **Certificates/standards:** passive energy building.

↑ | **Staircase**
↓ | **Section**

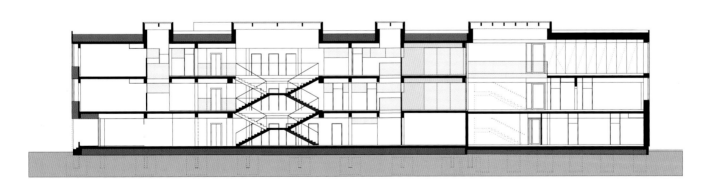

0   10   20 m

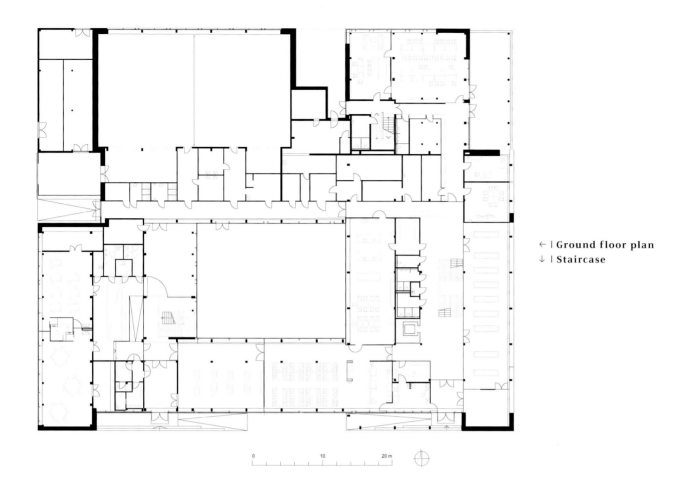

← | Ground floor plan
↓ | Staircase

0 10 20 m

Jourda Architectes

↑ | **South view,** from adjacent building

Mediacom 3
Saint-Denis

The project aims to reach basic office building goals, but does so with the optimal functionality and profitability. It also attempts to position itself as a unique object in a mixed setting. These standard goals come along with a special attention to sustainable development and the aim for the project to yield a zero energy office building. Due to great insulation and triple glazing, the annual operational energy consumption is just 41.65 kilowatt hours per square meter, balanced by the production of energy with photovoltaics in order to achieve zero energy standars. All sustainability criteria have been examined in order to promote a new type of architecture in the milieu of traditional office buildings.

Address: 31/33, rue du Landy, 93 200 Saint-Denis, France. **MEP engineer:** INEX Bet. **Client:** SCI Rue du Landy. **Completion:** 2010. **Ecological aspects:** solar energy; heat recovery; transmission heat loss U=0.12 W/m²K (walls), U=1.2 W/m²K (windows); triple glazed windows; high solar protections; rain-water reuse; natural ventilation in summer or spring. **Certificates/standards:** zero energy building, HQE label (high environmental quality), BBC label (low energy-consuming building).

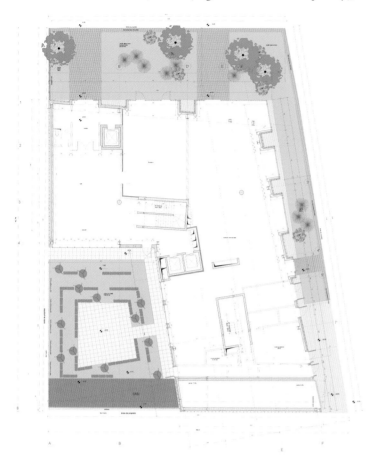

↑ | **Ground floor plan**
↓ | **East view,** perspective

↑ | **West view,** perspective

SFA
Simon Freie Architekten

↑ | **South view**
→ | **South-east view** at night

EN 65

Stuttgart

The loft house for highly mobile small families, singles or the young at heart is located on a south-facing cliff in the Bad-Cannstatt section of Stuttgart. Cubic service cells containing all necessary installations were created on the north side within the open layout plan. The living room area oriented to the south is completely flexible and can be left as a single room or subdivided into separate rooms using non-load bearing walls. The southern façade is completely glazed, and has projecting balconies which provide shade on summer afternoons. This method allows every apartment type to be created within the layout – from a loft to five-room apartments.

PROJECT FACTS

Address: Endersbacher Straße 65, 70374 Stuttgart, Germany. **Planning partner:** Struct-eng, Michael Fleck. **MEP engineer:** Truckenmüller & Partner, Wilhelm Schetter GmbH. **Client:** Andreas Schweickhardt. **Completion:** 2007. **Ecological aspects:** heat recovery; transmission heat loss $U=0.32$ W/m^{2}K; insulation glazing $U=0.7$ W/m^{2}K, triple glazed; ventilation engineering; 220 m^2 covered with greenery. **Degree of sealing:** 43%. **Certificates/standards:** KfW 60 Standard.

↑ | **Plans,** flexible floors
↙ | **Terrace**

← | **Restored basement**
↙ | **North view,** floor-to-ceiling French balconies

S, **M**, L, XL

SJB Architects /
Michael Bialek

↑ | **External view** from Albert Road
→ | **Aerial view** of roof terrace

The Szencorp Building
South Melbourne

The refurbishment project transformed an existing office building into an award-winning sustainable edifice, serving as a model for future redevelopment. It is the first Australian project to receive the 6 Green Star Award (Office Design V1) and to sign a 5-Star ABGR (NABERS) commitment agreement. Constraints posed by the existing building were overcome. A street presence was created using a screened façade which addresses solar shading and natural ventilation requirements. The center of the building contains a light-filled circulation space which filters light and air. Ceiling treatment combinations improved the internal volume and innovative sustainable technologies were incorporated in the surrounding outdoor spaces.

Address: 40 Albert Road, South Melbourne, Victoria, Australia, 3006. **Cybernetics/MEP engineer:** Connell Wagner. **Client:** Szencorp. **Completion:** 2005. **Ecological aspects:** solar energy; natural gas VRV A-C system; recycled timber; resistance to heat transmission R=1.23 (walls), R=1.75 (roof), R=1.05 (soffit); insulation glazing U=1.9 W/m²K; rainwater reuse; ventilation engineering. **Degree of sealing:** 72%. **Certificates/standards:** low energy building, Green Star Office Design (VI), 5-Star ABGR (NABERS).

← ← | **Meeting room**
↙ | **Reception**
← | **Façade**
↓ | **Floor plans**, ground level and level three

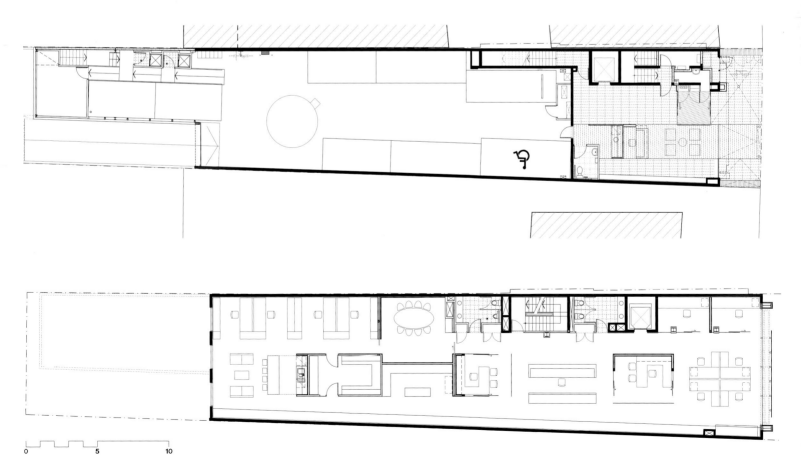

0   5   10

↑ | **Exterior view**
→ | **Side elevation**

Community Center Ludesch
Ludesch

In addition to creating a local focal point with a relation to the existing buildings, the con-cept for the community center included the construction of an ecological demonstration project. The new building is a compartment that is closed off on three sides and surrounds the new village square, created by added-on functions like stores, club rooms and the mu-nicipal office. During construction, a lot of attention was paid to avoid the use of toxic materials by using regional wood, renewable or recycled insulation materials and abstain-ing from PVC. The ventilation system is equipped with a ground water pump and allows customized climate control in all spaces resulting in minimum energy consumption.

PROJECT FACTS
Address: Raiffeisenstraße 56, 6713 Ludesch, Austria. **Cybernetics:** Bernhard Weithas. **MEP engineer:** Wilhelm Brugger. **Structural engineer:** Mader & Flatz Ziviltechniker, merz kaufmann partner. **Client:** City of Ludesch. **Completion:** 2005. **Ecological aspects:** solar energy; heat pumps; photovoltaic system; regrowing wood, sheepswool; sheepswool used for insulation; ventilation engineering. **Certificates/standards:** low/passive energy building.

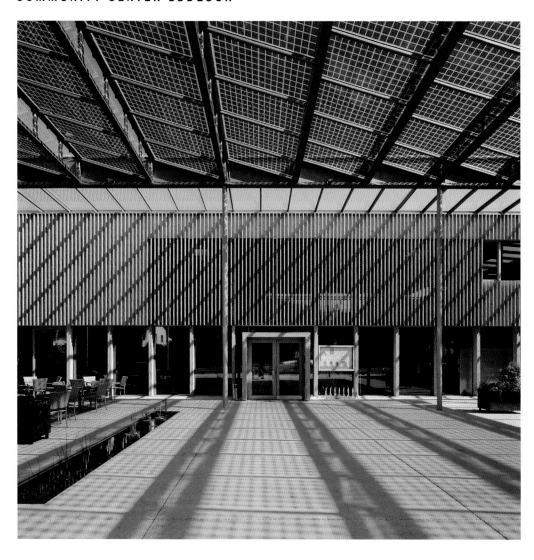

←← | **Wooden staircase** and façade
← | **Photovoltaic system** on the roof
↙ | **Wall,** horizontal section and vertical section
↓ | **Section**

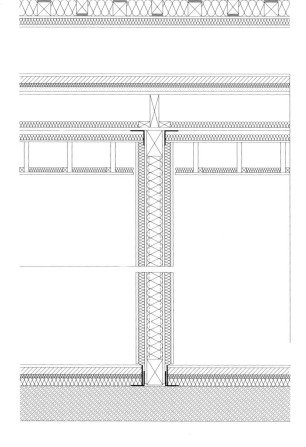

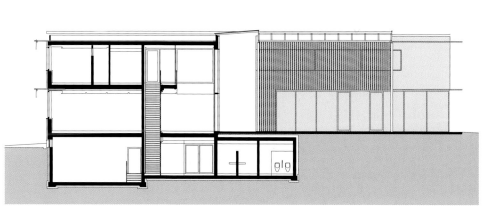

bhss – architekten /
Behnisch Hermus Schinko
Schumann

↑ | **Front elevation**
→ | **Covered balcony,** photovoltaic system

Headquarter Q-Cells SE
Bitterfeld-Wolfen

Q-Cells SE headquarters are located in Solar Valley, Europe's largest solar technology production facility between Berlin and Leipzig. The solar façades generate energy yields of
up to 150 kilowatts, which is then fed into the public grid. 300 closed photovoltaic modules constructed of glass additionally serve as transparent sun protection for 1,000 workspaces. Air delivery for meeting areas is heated using energy recovered from near-lying
production processes. Plastered capillary mats activate the building mass of the concrete
ceilings for cooling during warm seasons. Air from the cold side of the building is led
through the inner yard and used for window ventilation.

PROJECT FACTS

Address: Q-Cells SE, Sonnenallee, 06766 Bitterfeld, Germany. **General planner:** Hochtief Construction AG, Sachsen. **Cybernetics:** Ruffert & Partner. **MEP engineer:** Ingenieurbüro Balint, ZBP GmbH. **Client:** Q-Cells SE. **Completion:** 2009. **Ecological aspects:** solar energy; heat exchanger, waste heat recovery from production; plastered cooling ceilings; ventilation systems with cross flow plate heat exchanger; transmission heat loss H´T=1.33 W/m²K; insulation glazing U=1.1 W/m²K. **Degree of sealing:** 10%.

↑ | **Side elevation**
↓ | **Section**

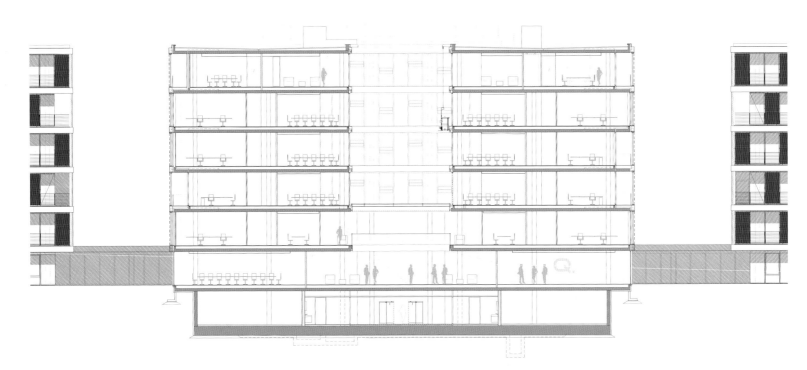

← | Photovoltaics
↓ | Covered balcony

Centola & Associati,
De8 Architetti / Mauro
Piantelli & Enrico Garbin

↑ | **Exterior view,** Grand Tour Borgo-hotel

Waterpower Amalfi Coast
City of Minori

Located in the context of the Amalfi Coast Unesco site, the project aims to recover a system of pre-industrial water mills currently in danger of collapse. The valley's hydropower, traditionally used in the production of Amalfi handmade paper and lemon irrigation is reinterpreted by the introduction of contemporary water systems that solve the current problems: accessibility and clean energy. The paper mills are reused for Grand Tour travelers, who can visit a public path with an Amalfi Marine Republic exhibition on the ground floor. The roofs are rebuilt with panels of artificial local stone and solar panels. A water powered funicular connects the nine floors and the public paths.

PROJECT FACTS

Address: Reginna Minor Valley, City of Minori, Italy. **Client:** City of Minori. **Completion:** 2012. **Ecological aspects:** solar energy, micro-hydroelectrical energy from the river; solar heat; recycled local stone; regrowing artificial stone; conversion of historical abandoned paper mills in danger of collapse. **Certificates/standards:** low energy building.

↑ | **Exterior view**
↓ | **Elevation**

↑ | **Exterior view,** spa and conference
↓ | **Floor plan**

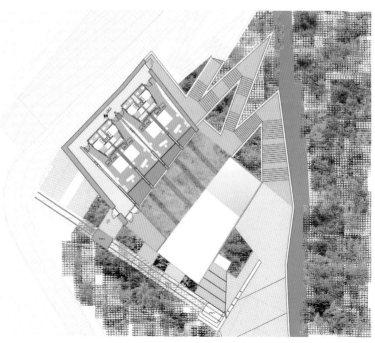

Kaden Klingbeil Architekten

↑ | **Courtyard façade**
→ | **Street façade**

e3

Berlin

The concept for the residential house in a densely populated Berlin quarter included the creation of living space with a high architectural appeal coupled with best possible environmental protection. A jamb-and-bar construction with braced solid wood walls acts as a load-bearing, space-defining, insulating and moisture-regulating structural element. Thanks to prefabrication and resulting shorter construction times compared to standard solid construction, primary energy consumption for the carcass was reduced by 30%. In addition, wood's excellent insulation properties help reduce the house's operational energy needs.

Address: Esmarchstraße 3, 10407 Berlin, Germany. **Structural engineer:** Prof. Natterer. **Client:** Baugruppe e3 Bau GbR. **Completion:** 2008. **Ecological aspects:** solar energy; solar heat; long-distance heating; regrowing wood; transmission heat loss U=0.42 W/m²K; airtightness 0.5; insulation glazing U=0.9 W/m²K; ventilation engineering; 300 m² covered with greenery; conversion flexibility due to absence of load-bearing walls and supports. **Degree of sealing:** 54%. **Certificates/standards:** KfW 60 Standard.

↑ | **Staircase**, third floor
← | **Isometry bare brickwork**

← | **Living room,** first floor
↓ | **Kitchen area,** fifth floor

↑ | **Rhythm of the roof**
↗ | **Front view**
→ | **Open passage** along the façade

Farm De Mikkelhorst

Haren

The program for the biological farm consists of several specific farming functions, combined with a few recreational facilities such as a teahouse, a shop, an educational space and a children's farm. The designers chose to bring all facilities under one continuous roof, providing a literal translation of the program. Within the clear and compact layout under the roof, the two areas can be easily distinguished: 'the house', a climatologically determined area in which all parts are established by architectural definitions, and 'the stable', the area with the farming functions. The designers let go of the layout of this second area – the 'farmer' gets a free hand here.

PROJECT FACTS

Address: Klaverlaan 37, 9753 BZ Haren, The Netherlands. **Cybernetics:** J. P. van de Weele. **Structural engineer:** Ingenieursbureau Wassenaar. **Client:** Stichting Ecologische Boerderij "De Mikkelhorst". **Completion:** 2003. **Ecological aspects:** solar energy; solar heat; central wood oven heat burning communal wood chips; floor heating using a low-temperature radiator; thermal zoning, recycled concrete of the former sewage plant; regrowing wood; sensor controlled automation; natural ventilation.

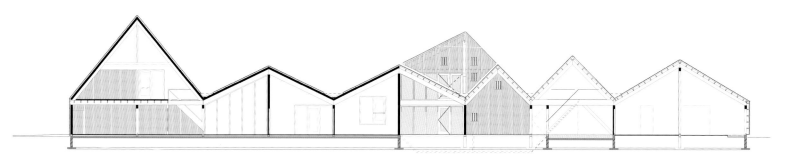

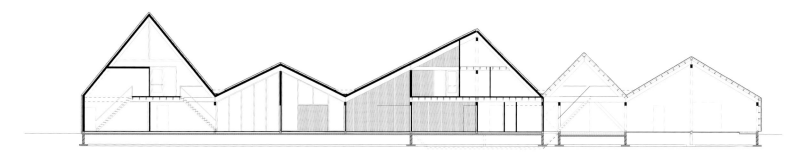

↑ | **Sections**
← | **Interior view**

← | Stable
↓ | Site plan

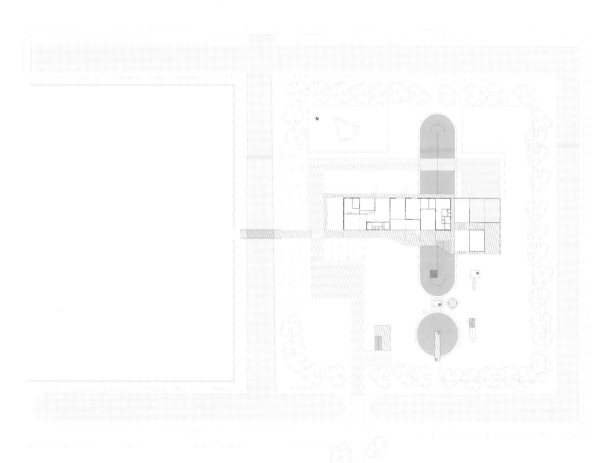

perraudinarchitectes

↑ | **Exterior view**
→ | **Entrance**

Solan Monastery Wine Storage

La Bastide d'Engras

Solid limestone from the Provence is the main building material used for the wine warehouse. It is ideally suited for wine storage and, being mined with a relatively low energy expenditure and with no application of chemicals, it is one of the most ecologically sound materials overall. Stone buildings are raised quickly, produce little waste at the site and their building material can be used again and again. The stone format of the two-story building, which was built by monks with their own labor, is standardized and the architecture concentrates on the essentials. Douglas fir roof beams reverberate the play of light and shade on the walls.

PROJECT FACTS

Address: 30330 La Bastide d'Engras, France. **Wood engineer:** Jacques Anglade. **Client:** Monastery of Solan. **Completion:** 2008. **Ecological aspects:** massive stone structure with high sustainability and longevity.

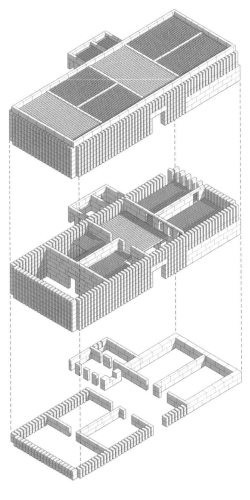

↖ | **New and old stone**
↑ | **Structure model**
← | **Elevation**

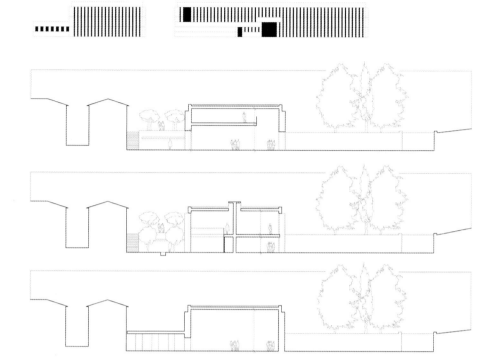

↖ | **Stones**, new and old
← | **Sections**
↓ | **Wine storage**

Croxton Collaborative
Architects

↑ I **Entrance area**
→ I **View from the bay**

Bay Educational Center
Providence

The Bay Education Center embodies the 'Save the Bay' mission to act as a steward of the
Narragansett Bay and its watershed. The horizontality of the coastal edge and water is an
inherent character of the site. The building reinforces this linear aspect by folding into
the land form. The arrival sequence opens to a panoramic view of the bay, culminating in
a dramatic south-facing entry sequence to the lobby. Mirroring the programmatic split,
the 4,572 square meter building is composed of two wings connected by a central lobby.
Public spaces are located to the south to maximize views and access to daylight, while support spaces are organized to the north against the berm.

PROJECT FACTS

Address: 100 Save The Bay Drive, Providence, RI 02905, USA. **Client:** Save The Bay, Inc. **Completion:** 2005. **Ecological aspects:** solar energy; 72 % reduction in peak electrical demand, 38 % reduction of carbon dioxide emissions; 20 kW photovoltaic array; insulation glazing; energyefficiency was obtained utilizing a blown-in insulation, viracon high performance glazing reduces total energy consumption by 10 %. **Certificates/standards:** low energy building, EPA "Phoenix" Award for Brownfield Redevelopment.

↑ | **Roof**
↓ | **Sections**
→ | **Interior view** of the lobby

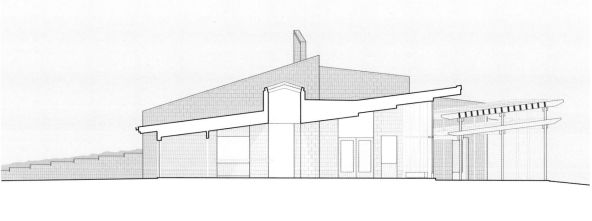

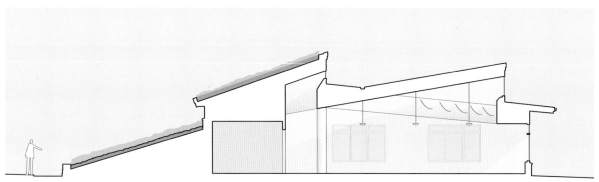

Skidmore, Owings & Merrill

↑ | **View from lakeside**
→ | **Front elevation**

Cathedral of Christ the Light

San Francisco

This religious building is an exemplary structure that uses traditional building materials translated into a modern language. The challenge of creating a building of a light and delicate character that is also earthquake-safe was met using glass and steel rod space frames. Wood, rather than steel, was used for the cathedral's supporting lattice because of its warmth and low construction costs. Using light as a central theme, the glass skin is composed of recently developed materials including ceramic fritted glass, which emanate prismatic effects and add tonal and line patterns for additional color and texture.

PROJECT FACTS

Address: 2121 Harrison Street, Oakland, CA 94612, USA. **Client:** Roman Catholic Diocese of Oakland. **Completion:** 2008. **Ecological aspects:** thermal inertia; ventilation engineering; covered with greenery; flexibility because of pre-fabrication of the wooden ribs, glass panes, and aluminum panels; longevity due to use of a friction-pendulum seismic base isolation system designed to withstand a 1000-year earthquake.

←← | **Nave** with altar and pantocrator
← | **Interior view**
↙ | **Ground floor plan**
↓ | **Exploded axis**

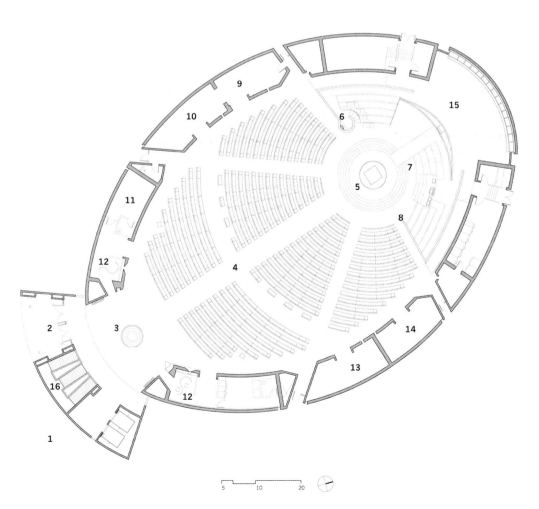

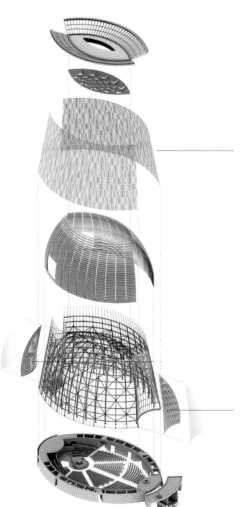

Kistelegdi Architecture
Office

↑ | **Main entrance** of the glass canopy
→ | **Glass hall,** double skin climate façade of the
thermal buffering zone

Modern Hungarian Gallery

Pécs

The first sustainable Hungarian museum presents objects as manifestations of the Transcendental and handles invisible energies in an artistic way: except for electricity, it is completely self-sufficient. The double skin façade of the glass hall allows enhanced thermal insulation and shell-cooling. Multifunctional 'energyspines' with columns incorporate vertical air and water distribution and include light deflection pipes for darker levels. Aerodynamically optimized 'air-birds' turn in the direction of prevailing winds. Their teardrop form allows improved air circulation which reduces the use of electricity. A geo-water system with a heat pump supplies thermoactive concrete slabs and a thermal micro network.

Address: Papnövelde Street 5, Pécs, Hungary. **Cybernetics:** Forródrót Kft. **MEP engineer:** H+V Bt., Szabolcs Vígh. **Client:** local government of Baranya County. **Completion:** 2010. **Ecological aspects:** wind energy (aerodynamical optimized 'air-birds'); heat reservoir, exchanger, pumps, recovery; thermoactive building systems; recycled Baroque building; energy consumption 100 kWh/m^2; winter garden as thermal buffering zone; rainwater reuse; ventilation engineering; 20 m^2 covered with greenery. **Degree of sealing:** 20%.

↖ | **Glass roof** with 'air-birds' for air supply and ventilation
↙ | **Main entrance** of museum courtyard

← | **Interior** with flexible service boxes
↓ | **Sections**

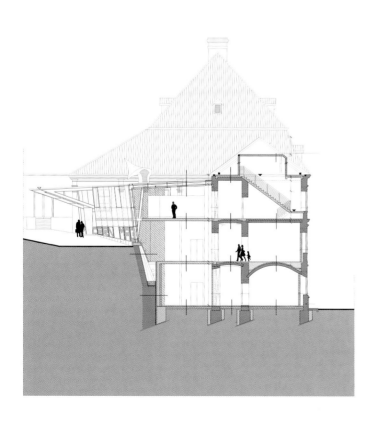

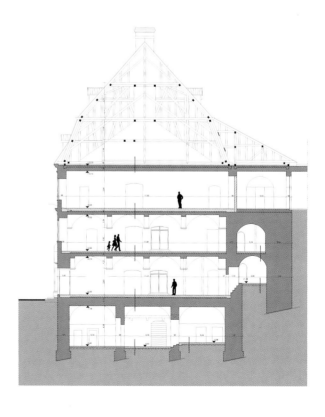

Large

Hermann Kaufmann

↑ | **View of residential complex** comprising
of clearly structured units
→ | **Front elevation**

Residences Mühlweg

Vienna

The buildings in the residential complex all have four stories, and in spite of differentiated tectonics, create a pleasant residential ambience with the help of their clear formal vocabulary. This is accented by the materialization of the façades using untreated larch wood in combination with colorful sliding panels. Heat is generated in a natural gas condensing boiler and conducted into apartments using a low-temperature heat network with a parallel pipes system. Water is heated using a thermal solar collector, which covers 50% of the demand. A central heat reservoir, heated by the solar collector, supplies the tap water distribution grid via an insulated circulation conduit.

PROJECT FACTS

Address: Mühlweg, 1020 Vienna, Austria. **MEP engineer:** s.d. & engineering, Pesek Planungsbüro, Holzforschung Austria. **Structural engineer:** merz kaufmann partner GmbH. **Landscape architect:** PlanSinn GmbH. **Client:** BWS Gemeinnützige Allgemeine Bau-, Wohn- und Siedlungsgen. Reg. Gen.m.b.H. **Completion:** 2006. **Ecological aspects:** solar energy; solar heat; regrowing wood; heating demand 36 kWh/m² annual. **Certificates/standards:** low energy building.

←← | Exterior view
← | South-east and south-west elevation

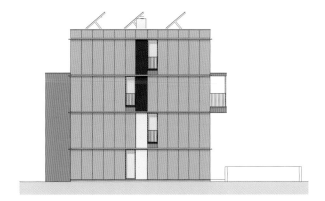

BVN Architecture /
Abbie Galvin, Laura Robinson, Sahra Embling

↑ | **Interior view**
→ | **Staircase**

Stockland Head Office

Sydney

Stockland Head Office addresses the challenge of sustainability through an innovative refurbishment of eight floors of an existing building to provide a lively environment that supports wellness and activity while reducing the office's environmental footprint. Key to this outcome is the eight-storey atrium which provides connectivity to all levels in a dynamic play of projecting floor planes, maximizing daylight, and improving access to views. The workplace is the first in Australia to achieve a 6 Star Green Star as built rating. The design focused on the health of human beings – fresh air in the workplace, daylight to work by, materials that are not toxic, and spaces that are humane.

PROJECT FACTS

Address: 133 Castlereagh Street, Sydney, NSW 2000, Australia. **Planning partner:** DEGW. **MEP engineer:** ARUP, VOS Group-engineers. **Client:** Stockland Trust Group. **Completion:** 2007. **Ecological aspects:** trigeneration plant; heat recovery; thermoactive building systems; recycled timber wall finish; low reflectivity, shading coefficient of 0.44; ventilation engineering; waterless urinals; inidividually switched lighting zones; CO_2 monitoring system. **Certificates/standards:** low energy building, 6 Star Green Star.

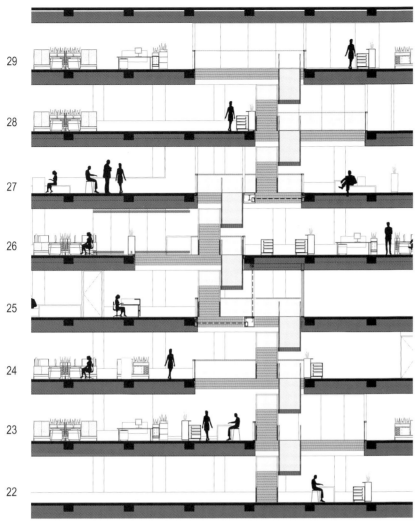

29

28

27

26

25

24

23

22

←←| Atrium
← | Section
↓ | Reception area

Behnisch Architects

↑ | **West façade,** main entrance
→ | **Atrium,** natural illumination of the atrium
using heliostats and mirrors

Genzyme Center
Cambridge, MA

The building embodies an ecological and social progress: A 12-story atrium which fulfils
the role of a climate oasis forks out like a tree with branches and twigs that reach from the
center of the layout to the outer façade. In this process it creates spatial situations with
various private and public identities. Gardens, terraces, walkways and squares combine to
create a variegated system of communication. The central space is illuminated with daylight using prisms and receives natural ventilation. The ventilation systems are controlled
by a Building Management System, but can be influenced by each user with the help of
open windows.

PROJECT FACTS

Address: 500 Kendall Street, Cambridge 02142, MA, USA. **Environmental consultant, MEP engineer:** Buro Happold. **Green Building/Leed Consultant:** Natural Logic. **Lighting:** LichtLabor Bartenbach. **Client:** Lyme Properties LLC, Genzyme Corp. **Completion:** 2004. **Ecological aspects:** solar energy; heat exchanger; warm water from cooling machinery condensation; waste heat from a power plant; air conditioning glass atrium; rainwater reuse; optimum daylight exploitation by heliostats. **Certificates/standards:** LEED Platinum 2005.

↑ | **Entrance garden**
↙ | **Floor plan**, fifth floor
↓ | **Sketch**

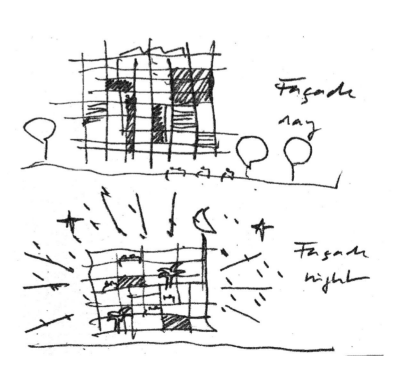

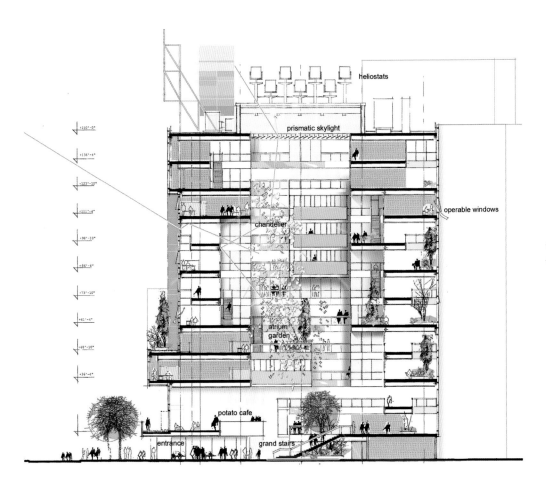

+150'-0"
+136'-4"
+123'-10"
+111'-4"
+98'-10"
+86'-4"
+73'-10"
+61'-4"
+48'-10"
+36'-4"

heliostats

prismatic skylight

operable windows

chandelier

atrium
garden

potato cafe

entrance

grand stairs

← | **North section**
↓ | **Law library**, level 10

CO Architects

↑ | **Terrace** with view to the desert landscape
→ | **One of the pavilions,** entrance area

Peter and Paula Fasseas Cancer Clinic

Tucson

An abandoned facility was gutted to bring desert gardens, natural light and sweeping Arizona vistas to patients and staff. Three window-lined garden courtyards, deeply incised into the floor plates, transform a cavernous, dark structure into one with abundant natural light and mountain views. Additions to the existing facility included a new front entrance containing a recessed porch under a protective canopy. The trellises on the east and west sides of the building give it light and shadow and also visually extend the interior to the outside. The desert gardens include an arroyo to collect rainwater and condense moisture from the clinic's air-conditioning system.

PROJECT FACTS
Address: 3838 N Campbell Avenue, Tucson, AZ 85719, USA. **Client:** University Medical Center, University of Arizona. **Completion:** 2007. **Ecological aspects:** thermoactive building systems; airtightness; insulation glazing; rainwater reuse; complete building automation; 10,220 m² covered with greenery; native landscaping requiring little or no irrigation.

↑ | Main entrance
← | Site plan

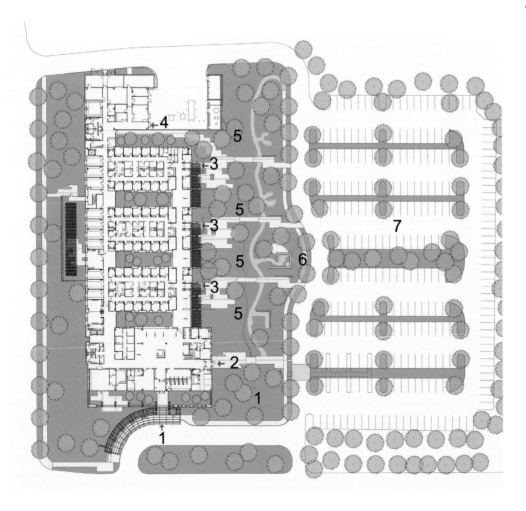

← ↓ | **Desert gardens** bring natural light and garden views to corridors and patient care areas

Jo Coenen & Co

↑ | **View on workstations** along the void
→ | **Southern façade**

Central Library
Amsterdam

The new city library will be the centerpiece of the Oosterdokseiland, a redeveloped area in Amsterdam. The assignment is an accumulated program of 28,500 square meters in an urban envelope with a volume of about 40 meters in height, 40 meters in width and 120 meters in length. The library was designed as an interior meeting place and an easily discernable landmark in the Amsterdam townscape. Form, function and technique are inextricably linked. The materialization of the exterior (natural stone) continues within the materialization of the interior. The library is one of the three European ECO buildings and received the Amsterdam's most Durable Public Building Award in 2008.

PROJECT FACTS

Address: Oosterdoksstraat 110, 1011 DK Amsterdam, The Netherlands. **Client:** City of Amsterdam. **Completion:** 2007. **Ecological aspects:** solar energy; solar heat; heat reservoir, pumps; thermo-active building systems; environmentally friendly concrete used for thermoactive slabs, FSC certified wood WRC; heat consumption and related CO_2 emission cut by 35–50%; HR++ glass; ventilation engineering. **Certificates/standards:** low energy building, ECO building Certificate.

↑ | **Periodicals section**
← | **Deep window cases**

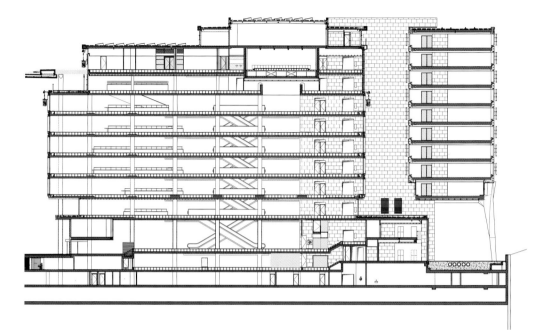

← | South-north cross section
↓ | Children's section

↑ | **Bird's-eye view**
→ | **Façade,** different materials and colors create a vivid countenance

The California Endowment

Los Angeles

The design for the California Endowment, a charitable organization situated at the heart of downtown Los Angeles, creates an urban garden, a community meeting center and 3,962 square meters of sustainable office space. The different edifices of the complex are constructed to relate to the surrounding contexts. Sustainability goals were included in the project, among them reduction of energy consumption, energy efficient design and use of recycled and recyclable materials. The campus has also been developed to provide a healthy work environment, for instance exhibiting strong daylight penetration in order to create light and vivid spaces while reducing energy consumption.

PROJECT FACTS

Address: 1000 N. Alameda Street, Los Angeles, CA 90012, USA. **Client:** The California Endowment. **Completion:** 2006. **Ecological aspects:** insulation glazing; rainwater reuse; complete building automation; ventilation engineering. **Certificates/standards:** ASLA/SCC Institutional Honor Award 2007, American Society of Landscape Architects Southern California Council; Civic Architectural Award 2007, Los Angeles Business Council; Building Team of the Year 2007, American Institute of Architects, Los Angeles Chapter.

↖ | **View** of the campus
↑ | **Communal spaces**
← | **View** from the street

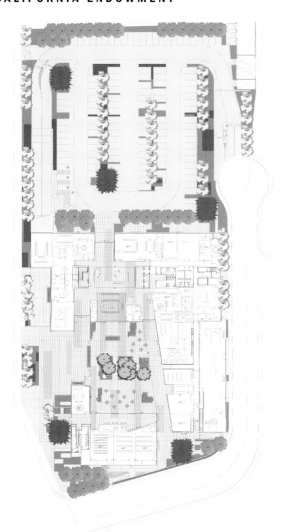

← | **Site plan** with ground floor
↓ | **Interior view,** bright office spaces

Bucholz McEvoy Architects

↑ | **Aerial view**
↗ | **Offices / conference center**
→ | **Day clinic and hotel**

Elm Park

Low energy mixed-use development, Dublin

This project offers the possibility of a new type of urban environment in Dublin, one which is firmly lodged in its natural environment, while fine-tuned to energy conservation and generation and the functional potential of its components. It is a large, functionally diverse ensemble of elements integrated into a continuous energy-balanced piece of urban landscape. It is a place where buildings are oriented so as to minimize their energy demand and maximize their use of natural light, where landscape facilitates movement, creates connections between activities and people, provides a place of density and concentration, for people to live, work, and engage in leisure.

PROJECT FACTS

Address: Merrion Road, Dublin 4, Ireland. **Environmental engineer:** Transsolar Energietechnik. **Client:** Radora Developments. **Completion:** 2008. **Ecological aspects:** solar, wind, woodchip biomass energy; combined heat and power generation system; regrowing timber. **Certificates/standards:** Green Awards 2008 (finalist), OPUS Award 2008, Good Design is Good Business Award 2008, RIAI Award 2008.

↖ | **The long-span structural elements** are engineered as supports of the breathing façades
← | **Canopy construction** over the courtyards
↓ | **Wind forces** are used to drive the natural ventilation strategy

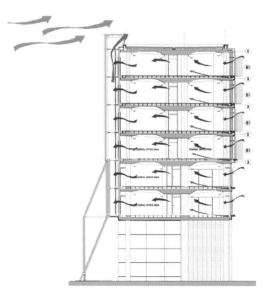

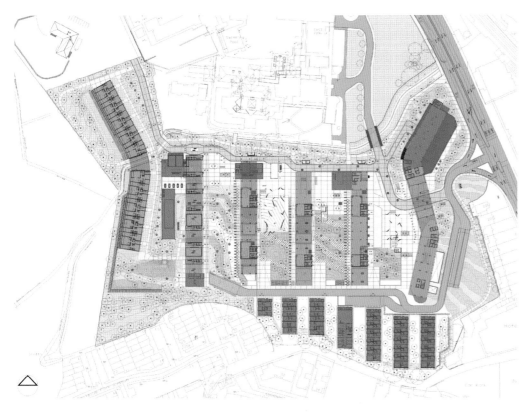

← | Site plan
↓ | Section
↓↓ | Apartment buildings

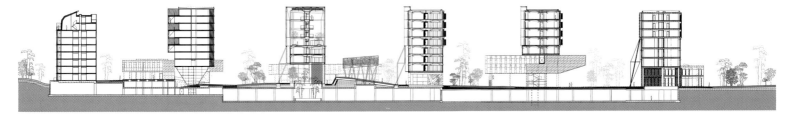

T. R. Hamzah & Yeang /
Dr. Ken Yeang, Mitchell
Gelber, Esther Klausen,
Faizah Rahmat

↑ | **Exterior view**

Solaris

Singapore

The project is a multi-tenant facility for info-comm, media, science and engineering research located at the Fusionopolis development within the 'one-north' masterplan by Zaha
Hadid Architects. A flagship project, it will become a vibrant focal point for the 'one-north'
community through the introduction of open interactive spaces, creative use of skylights
and courtyards for natural light and ventilation, cascading landscaped terraces and roof
gardens, and a continuous landscaped spiral ramp, an extension of 'one-north' Park across
the street, linking an escalating sequence of sky parks which interpenetrate the building's
façade. By way of its various ecological features and innovative vertical green concept, the
building strives to enhance the site's existing ecosystems, rather than replacing them.

PROJECT FACTS

Address: Ayer Rajah Avenue, Singapore 138666, Singapore. **Planning partner:** CPG Consultants Pte Ltd. **Client:** Soilbuild Group Holdings Ltd. **Completion:** 2010. **Ecological aspects:** solar shading devices; district cooling plant; recycled TBD; insulation glazing using double glazed Low-E façade system; rainwater reuse; complete building automation; ventilation engineering; 9,000 m² covered with greenery. **Certificates/standards:** low energy building, Singapore GreenMark Platinum Rating (candidate).

↑ | **Aerial view,** extensive green roof system
↓ | **Diagram,** showing the 1.5 km continuous landscaped spiral ramp

↓ | **Diagram,** showing the design concept of the escalating sequence of roof terraces

Cambridge Seven
Associates

↑ | **Expansion entry** with oversized elevator
→ | **North-west façade** along Harborwalk

Boston Children's Museum

Boston

The expansion and renovation reinforces the museum's position as one of America's premier institutions for families and as a world-class visitor destination. The addition to the existing wool storage warehouse embraces the dramatic waterfront site in the historic Fort Point Channel District, and provides a vibrant and inviting urban space. A new approach to the building and public access to the water's edge reinvigorate the visitor's experience. With the incorporation of large parts of the existing building structure into the design, a responsible choice of materials and energy efficient technologies, the Boston Children's Museum became the first LEED Gold certified museum in Boston.

PROJECT FACTS

Address: 300 Congress Street, Boston, MA 02210, USA. **MEP engineer:** R. G. Vanderweil. **Landscape architect:** Van Valkenburgh Associates Inc. **Sustainable design:** The Green Roundtable, Inc. **Client:** Boston Children's Museum. **Completion:** 2007. **Ecological aspects:** heat pumps, heat recovery; recycled timbers from existing warehouse; recycled marble boulders; insulated glazing: Low-E coating; rainwater reuse; 480 m² green roof. **Certificates/standards:** LEED Gold, Green Power Certificates.

↑ | **North elevation,** recycled timber storytelling podium, exterior wood and zinc rain screen
↓ | **Ground floor plan**

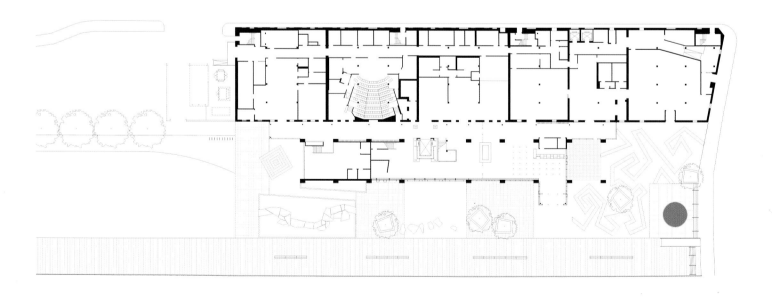

← | **Curtain wall and rain screen façade,**
wood rain screen, removable zinc sun control panels
↓ | **Main lobby** with recycled timber information
desk and climbing structure by Lucky Climbers LLC

Zoltán Bachman, Bálint Bachmann, István Kistelegdi, Ákos Hutter

↑ | **View from south-east,** double skin climate façade
→ | **Diverse facilities** included in the complex

PTE Science Building

Pécs

The eco-research complex is a prototype research project in itself, heating and cooling its space completely with geothermic seasonal storage. Heat pumps and 100 boreholes accumulate summer heat and winter cold in two sections of soil at a depth of 100 meters. The building can activate concrete cores with stored energy from millions of cubic meters of soil. Energy consumption is minimal because of the low temperature level. An ancient method combined with modern multi-skin façades pre-cools fresh air in the climate skin with aqua adiabatic elements; heat pumps generate end-cooling. Water elements change the energy storage ability of the aqua-skin façade, while blocking and deflecting light, behaving as an intelligent organism.

PROJECT FACTS
Address: Ifjúság Street, Hrsz: 2917/1, Pécs, Hungary. **Cybernetics:** Forródrót Kft. **MEP engineer:** H+V Bt., Szabolcs Vígh, SMG-SISU Engineering Consulting, Gábor Szígyártó. **Client:** University Pécs PTE. **Completion:** 2011. **Ecological aspects:** solar, wind energy; 100-meter deep geothermal boreholes; double layer climate skin research-façade; heat pump circulation systems; thermoactive building systems; energy consumption 144 kWh/m²; greenhouses; rainwater reuse. **Degree of sealing:** 7.6 %.

↑ | **Bird's-eye view**
← | **Cross section**

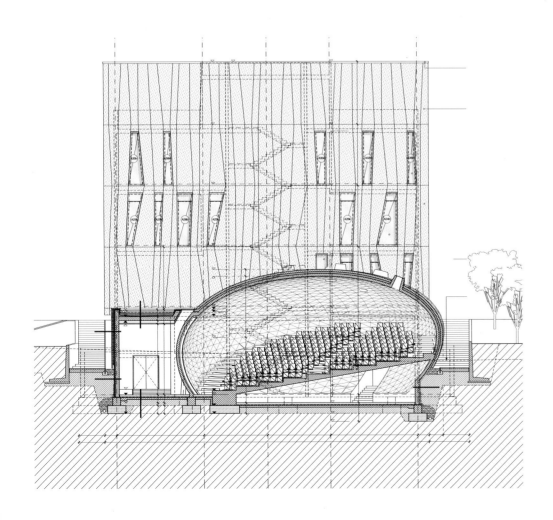

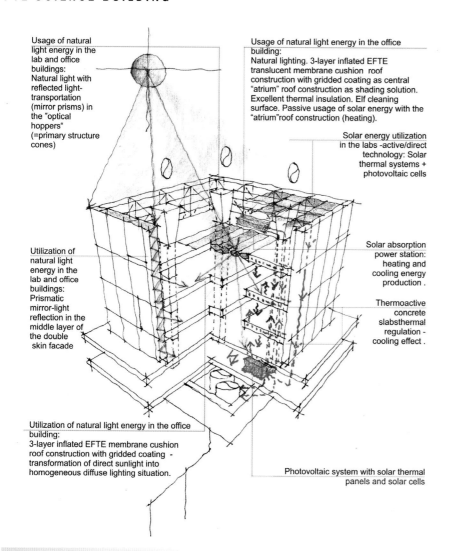

Usage of natural light energy in the lab and office buildings: Natural light with reflected light-transportation (mirror prisms) in the "optical hoppers" (=primary structure cones)

Usage of natural light energy in the office building: Natural lighting. 3-layer inflated EFTE translucent membrane cushion roof construction with gridded coating as central "atrium" roof construction as shading solution. Excellent thermal insulation. Elf cleaning surface. Passive usage of solar energy with the "atrium" roof construction (heating).

Solar energy utilization in the labs -active/direct technology: Solar thermal systems + photovoltaic cells

Utilization of natural light energy in the lab and office buildings: Prismatic mirror-light reflection in the middle layer of the double skin facade

Solar absorption power station: heating and cooling energy production .

Thermoactive concrete slabsthermal regulation - cooling effect .

Utilization of natural light energy in the office building: 3-layer inflated EFTE membrane cushion roof construction with gridded coating - transformation of direct sunlight into homogeneous diffuse lighting situation.

Photovoltaic system with solar thermal panels and solar cells

← | **Sketch,** natural light deflection and direct, active solar technology
↓ | **East view,** science building's silhouette

↑ | **View from north**
→ | **Façade**

C&A Eco-Store

Mainz

Energy optimization in concert with optical improvement have been achieved in the course of a comprehensive rehabilitation of the warehouse. In addition to reduction of heating energy and electricity consumption, it was also possible to achieve CO_2 emission-free operation. The existing façade was optically and technically optimized using stainless steel webbing. It was taken care to use recycled materials whenever possible, and value was placed on recyclability of individual components. Enhanced insulation properties were achieved by improvement of façade and roof and implementation of heat-absorbing windows.

PROJECT FACTS

Address: Seppel-Glückert-Passage, 55116 Mainz, Germany. **Client:** Redevco Services Deutschland GmbH. **Completion:** 2008. **Ecological aspects:** solar, water energy; heat exchanger, recovery; partial air conditioning with separate mixed air and zone regulation; 30% under EnEV (walls); insulation glazing; ventilation engineering. **Certificates / standards:** 43% under EnEV 2007, BREEAM (first European certified renovation, classified 'very good').

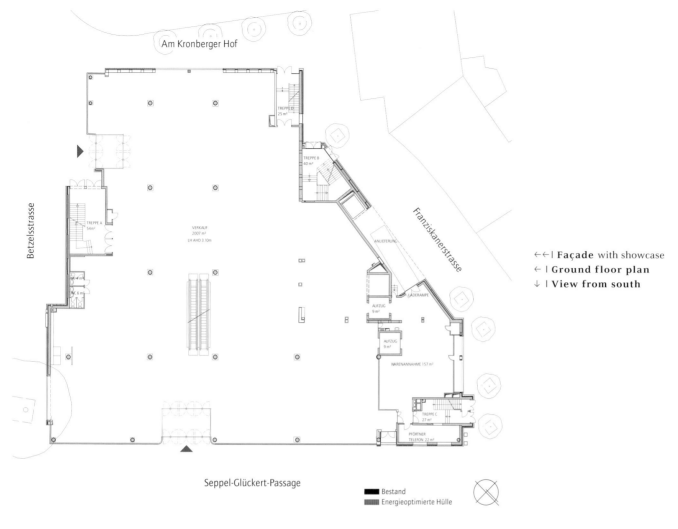

Am Kronberger Hof

Betzelsstrasse

Franziskanerstrasse

TREPPE D
25 m²

TREPPE B
40 m²

TREPPE A
54m²

VERKAUF
2007 m²
LH AHD 3.10m

ANLIEFERUNG

ALFZUG
9 m²

LADERAMPE

AUFZUG
9 m²

WARENANNAHME 157 m²

TREPPE C
27 m²

PFÖRTNER
TELEFON 22 m²

Seppel-Glückert-Passage

←← | **Façade** with showcase
← | **Ground floor plan**
↓ | **View from south**

Bestand
Energieoptimierte Hülle

Enota

↑ | **Entrance**
→ | **Terrace**

Hotel Sotelia
Podčetrtek

Hotel Sotelia fills the gap between two existing hotels. During the design process, the primary concern was to avoid creating an immense building mass which would have blocked the last remaining view of the forest. The volume is broken up into small units arranged in landscape-hugging tiers. As a result, the four-story building appears much lower and smaller. The specific shape of the hotel was dictated by the folds in the landscape and is able to offer passers-by a strong spatial experience. The front of the building is perceived as a two-dimensional set composed of parallel planes placed one behind the other. A walk around the hotel reveals entirely different views of the timber façade.

PROJECT FACTS

Address: Zdraviliška cesta 24, 3254 Podčetrtek, Slovenia. **Landscape architect:** Bruto. **Client:** Terme Olimia. **Completion:** 2006. **Ecological aspects:** geothermal energy; heat recovery; thermoactive building systems; insulation glazing; complete building automation; ventilation engineering; 4,725 m² covered with greenery. **Degree of sealing:** 60%.

↑ | **Exterior**
← | **Façade detail**

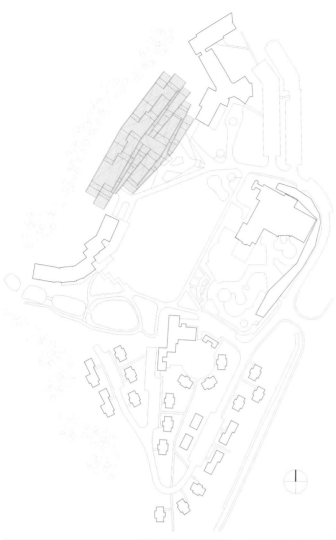

← | Situation
↓ | Entrance area

Massimiliano e Doriana
Fuksas

↑ | **On the roof**
↗ | **Emerging glass skin**
→ | **Perspective**

PalaisQuartier –
Shopping Center MyZeil

Frankfurt/Main

The shopping and entertainment area is part of an urban development project located at the heart of the city of Frankfurt. The entire mall functions as an in-between space separating the exterior and the shops. Instead of air conditioning, floor heating and cooling is used throughout the mall. The interior temperature is moderate, but fluctuates between summer and winter use to reduce energy consumption. The steel used on the roof and façades is reusable and the construction allows dismantling of most parts for recycling. Exposure to daylight is made possible through the glass skin, which greatly helps reduce the energy need for illumination.

PROJECT FACTS

Address: Zeil, Frankfurt/Main, Germany. **Structural engineer:** Knippers-Helbig, Krebs und Kiefer. **Client:** palais quartier GmbH & Co. KG. **Completion:** 2009. **Ecological aspects:** geothermal energy; thermoactive building systems; heat storage; hybrid coolers; insulation glazing $U=1.2$ W/m²K, g-value $=0.3$; $U=0.28$ W/m²K printed glass to minimize energy gain; rainwater reuse; ventilation engineering. **Certificates/standards:** low energy building.

↑ | **Front elevation**
← | **Fourth floor plan**

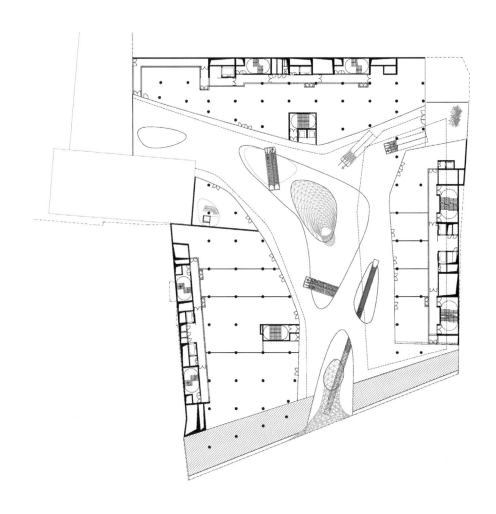

↑ | Interior view
↓ | Roof construction

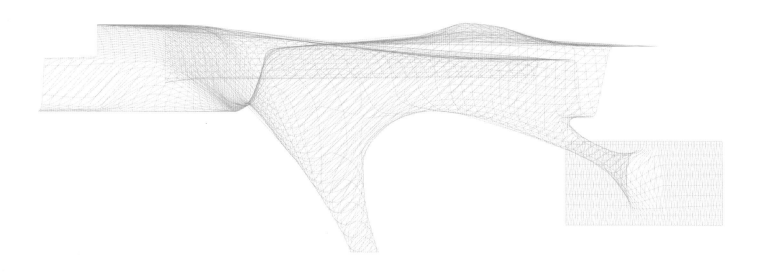

↑ | **Aerial view**

New Government Quarter
Budapest

The project intends to turn a symbol of power into an exemplary model of common sense, responsibility and sustainability. Integrated concepts of energy, architecture and urbanism make this urban development a convincing example for the nation as a whole, providing clear, long-term benefits for the community. Minute details about the project will be published on the Internet to provide a democratic access to information and increase accountability. Contextual concerns played a major role in the project. To exploit the energy created by the emergence of such a large and important building, an extensive urban rehabilitation is planned.

PROJECT FACTS

Address: Budapest, Hungary. **Client:** State of Hungary. **Ecological aspects:** solar, wind energy, green electricity; solar heat; heat reservoir, exchanger, pumps, recovery; thermoactive building systems; PCM wall plaster; air ground collector; transmission heat loss 2.3 MW with $qm=0.104$ W/m^{3}K; insulation glazing U=1.2 W/m^{2}K; plant houses, green fence; rainwater reuse; complete building automation; ventilation engineering; 20.25 m^2 covered with greenery. **Degree of sealing:** 63 %. **Certificates/standards:** zero energy building.

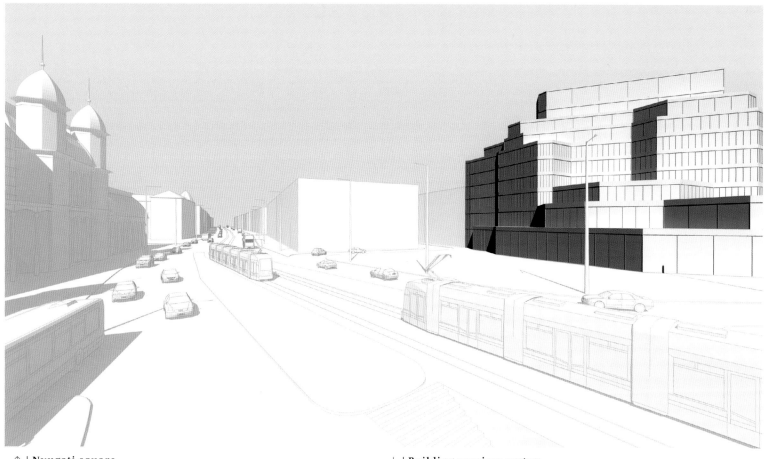

↑ | **Nyugati square**
↓ | **System** of horticultural surface
↓↓ | **System** of inner courtyards

↓ | **Building services system**

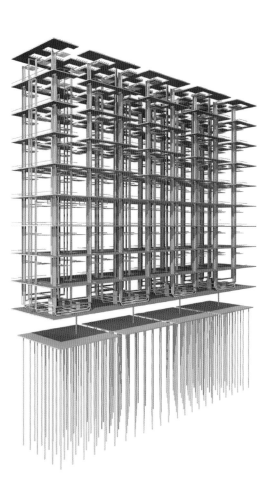

↑ | **Exterior view**

Federal Environmental Agency
Dessau

The new building housing the Federal Environmental Agency takes up multiple measures to limit energy use and carbon dioxide exhaust, combining these in an architecture that is economical, but still stimulates the senses. Dessau's derelict gas quarter has been selected as the location for sustainable urban planning. Contaminated areas were rehabilitated and existing train station and factory buildings were integrated into the complex. The compact overall form, outer wall insulation, selection of ecologically worthwhile building materials as well as the employment of a photovoltaic system and a large geothermal energy exchange system all contribute to the structure's sustainability.

PROJECT FACTS
Address: Am Wörlitzer Platz, 1, 06844 Dessau, Germany. **MEP engineer:** Zibell Willner & Partner.
Structural engineer: Krebs & Kiefer, Berlin. **Landscape architect:** ST raum a. **Client:** State of Germany.
Completion: 2005. **Ecological aspects:** solar energy; solar heat; heat exchanger, recovery; thermoactive
building systems; over current elements; rainwater reuse; ventilation engineering; roof covered with
greenery. **Degree of sealing:** 46%. **Certificates/standards:** low/passive energy building, DGNB Gold.

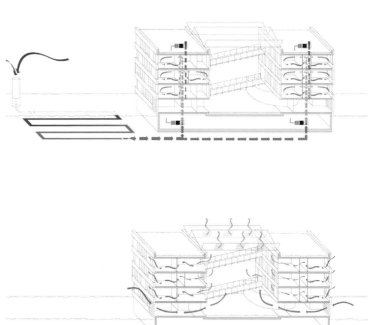

↑ | **View into atrium**
↓ | **Elevation**

↑↑ | **Air conditioning winter,** day
↑ | **Air conditioning summer,** night

↑ | **Façade** with climbing wall and photovoltaic
elements
→ | **Climbing wall**

Paul-Horn-Arena

Tübingen

The idea of the sports hall is based on the concept of a multifunctional arena and two characteristics: maximum exploitation qualities together with design that is unusual for sports
facilities. A giant, modern climbing wall acts as the northwestern façade. The southwest-
ern façade, with its entire surface formed by photovoltaic modules, generates up to 30,000
kilowatt hours of clean electricity that is fed into the public grid. The hall is ventilated
using a concrete channel buried underground, where air is cooled in the summer and kept
warm in the winter. The heating system of a neighboring swimming hall provides heat via
a local heat bond, which results in it being used in a more effective way.

PROJECT FACTS

Address: Europastraße 50, 72072 Tübingen, Germany. **MEP engineer:** Interplan Gebäudetechnik. **Client:** University of the City of Tübingen. **Completion:** 2004. **Ecological aspects:** solar energy; solar heat; heat exchanger, recovery; air supply pre-conditioning via an underground conduit; recycled vegetation layer for the green roof; insulation glazing U=1.1 W/m²K; complete building automation; 2,500 m² covered with greenery; longevity due to reinforced concrete. **Degree of sealing:** 42%.

↑ | **Façade** with photovoltaic elements
↓ | **Elevation and longitudinal section**

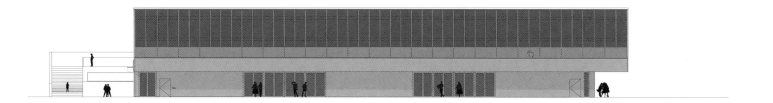

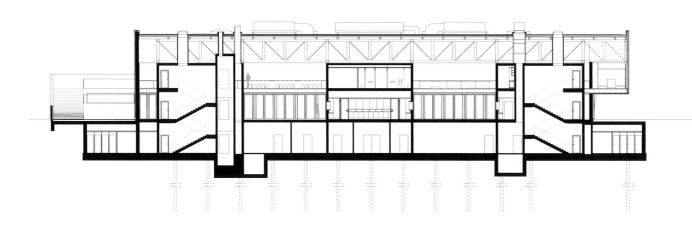

← | **Façade** with streetball area
↓ | **Interior view**

Prof. Christoph Mäckler
Architekten

↑ | **Foyer**
→ | **View from Opernplatz**

OpernTurm
Frankfurt/Main

The new building reinstates the original metropolitan setting to the Frankfurt Opera ensemble by picking up on the peripheral development height and 19th century materiality. Behind, the OpernTurm rises 170 meters into the air. Instead of being clad with the conventional glass façades, this is the first German tower of its size to have a façade completely out of natural stone. The light Portuguese sandstone harmonizes with the Old Opera building. The sustainable construction method succeeds because it respects simple ground principles: more than half of the façade is closed. In combination with a highly efficient glazing, this significantly reduces the solar factor.

PROJECT FACTS

Address: Bockenheimer Landstraße 2–4, 60306 Frankfurt/Main, Germany. **Planning partner:** BGS, Ebener & Partner, B+G, BPK, LichtVision, Jappsen Ingenieure. **MEP engineer:** TechDesign. **Client:** Tishman Speyer. **Completion:** 2009. **Ecological aspects:** district heating; heat exchanger, recovery; thermoactive building systems; insulation glazing U=1.1 W/m²K; ventilation engineering; 5,500 m² covered with green. **Degree of sealing:** 41%. **Certificates/standards:** 23% under EnEV 2007, LEED Gold (candidate).

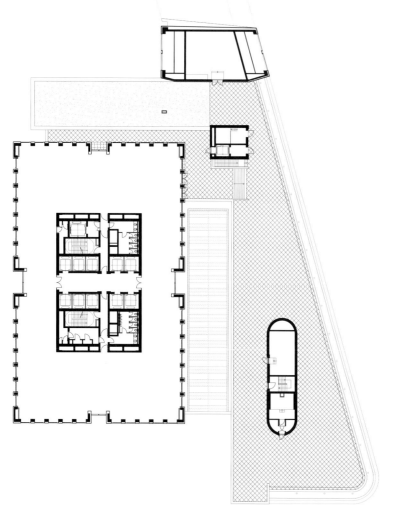

↑ | **Elevation** Bockenheimer Landstraße /
Bockenheimer Anlage
← | **Typical floor plan** with platform
↓ | **Section**

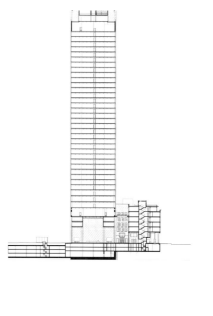

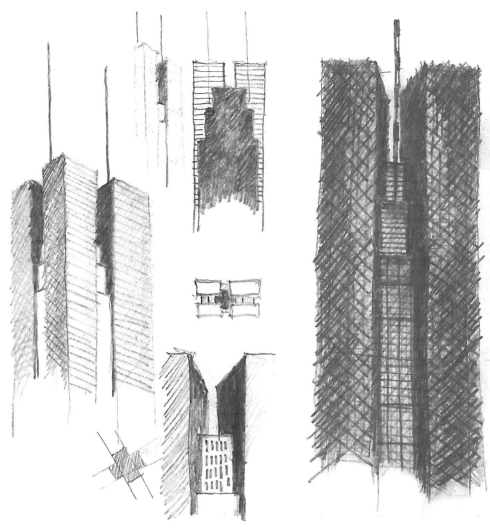

← | **Sketches**
↓ | **Skyline** at night

Bétrix & Consolascio
Architekten
with Eric Maier, Erwin Gruber

↑ | **Façade**
↗ | **Bird's-eye view**, solar panels
→ | **View of the grandstands**

Letzigrund Stadium

Zurich

Above its historical significance, the new stadium plays a key urban planning role as an open infrastructure. The roof surface is extensively greened and a 250 kilowatt photovoltaic collector system (without the customary elevation and with only a 5% slant due to optical concerns) feed about 184,000 kilowatt hours into the public grid. The building mass of the old stadium was broken down into components, sorted and recycled. Circa 90% of the old construction materials were reused as recycled concrete, scrap iron, recycled glass or fuel for a heating plant. Even the excavation from the deeper-lying playing field was to a large extent reused on site for the new building.

PROJECT FACTS

Address: Badenerstrasse 500, 8048 Zurich, Switzerland. **Planning partner:** Walt & Galmarini AG. **Client:** City of Zurich. **Completion:** 2007. **Ecological aspects:** solar, wood pellets energy; 75% renewable energy; solar heat; pellets oven; regrowing wood; transmission heat loss Minergie standard; airtightness Minergie standard; insulation glazing U=1.1 W/m²K; 18,500 m² covered with greenery. **Degree of sealing:** 32%. **Certificates/standards:** Minergie.

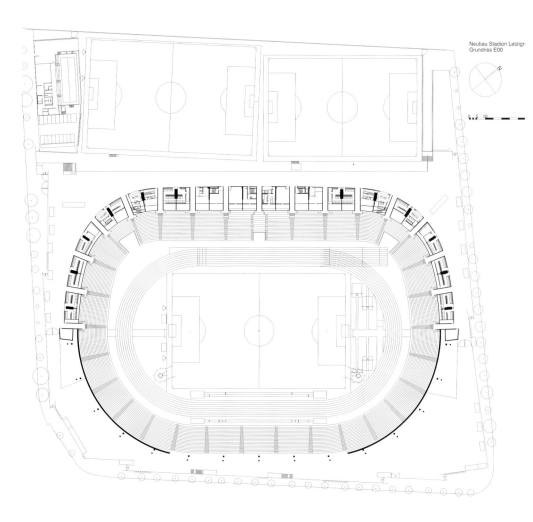

Neubau Stadion Letzigr
Grundriss E00

←← | **View of the ramp**
↙ | **'Dancing' stilts**
← | **Ground floor plan**
↓ | **Snack bar** in front of the ramp

Centola & Associati /
Luigi Centola

↑ | **General concept 1**, renaturalization and algae cultivations
↗ | **General concept 2**, renaturalization and bioplantations
→ | **General concept 3**, renaturalization and urban gardens

BioVallo
Vallo di Diano

The project is composed of a single masterplan that encompasses 13 subordinate projects for reuse and renaturalization of 70 abandoned quarries in the Vallo di Diano Unesco Site. Commissioned by the mountain community, BioVallo is a permanent exhibition at the Certosa di Padula. The network of programs for the quarries is complex with many different complementary ideas and uses in order to build a new 'Green Economy' for a neglected, beautiful area. The Innovation Pavilion is the BioVallo info-point, displaying all technologies used for the renaturalization of the site. The pavilion skin consists of translucent bioplastic filled with water and algae.

PROJECT FACTS

Address: Vallo di Diano, Unesco Site, Italy. **Sustainability:** Savener. **Landscape architect:** Proap. **Client:** Comunità Montana Vallo di Diano. **Completion:** 2010. **Ecological aspects:** solar, wind, micro-aeolian, micro-hydroelectrical, micro-photovoltaic energy; solar heat; rainwater reuse. **Certificates / standards:** zero energy building.

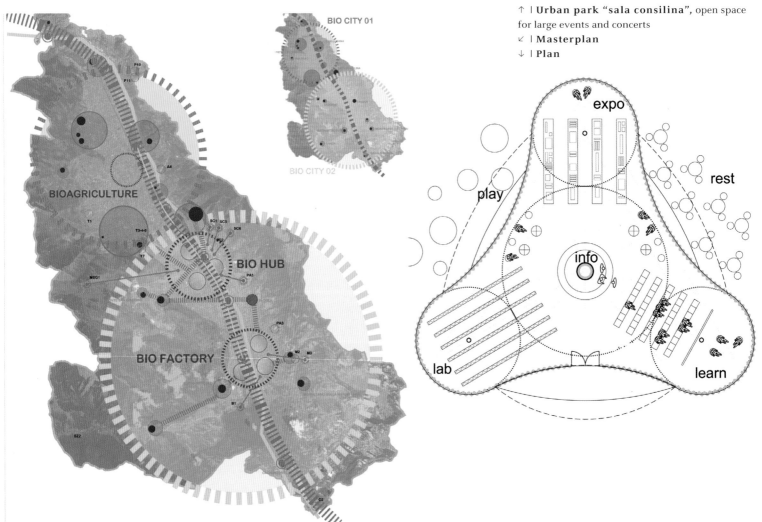

↑ | **Urban park "sala consilina",** open space for large events and concerts
↙ | **Masterplan**
↓ | **Plan**

← | **Cultural garden "atena lucana",** terraces with the botanical systems of Vallo di Diano
↙ | **Sections and elevation**

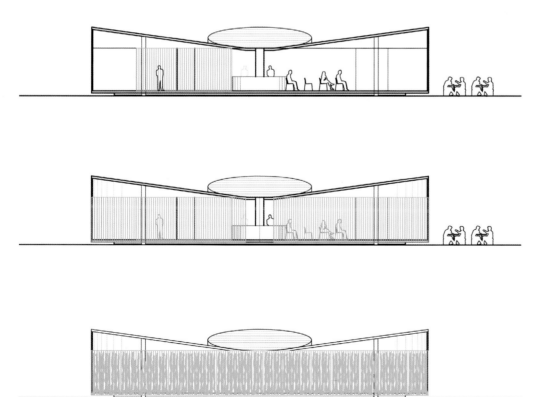

↑ | **Aerial view**
→ | **Shaded gardens** flanking the terminals

Suvarnabhumi International Airport

Bangkok

Openness and orientation in large spaces is architecturally important to airport planning. The motion suggested by the roof and layout must create memorable images and blur boundaries between public and private space. Fulfillment of all these qualities make an airport terminal a 'mini-city'. The resulting building sports wide-spanning, lightweight steel structures, exposed pre-cast concrete elements, clear or Low-E coated glass, a three-layer translucent membrane, and integrated cooling system that uses water as a low energy carrier, concrete core activation and a displacement ventilation system with minimal air exchange. These components and parts maximize daylight and comfort, yet minimize the use of energy.

PROJECT FACTS

Address: Suvarnabhumi International Airport, Bangkok, Thailand. **Planning partner:** ACT Consultants. **Climate and Environmental Concept:** Transsolar Energietechnik. **MEP engineer:** Flack + Kurtz. **Structural engineer:** Werner Sobek Ingenieure. **Lighting Art:** Yann Kersalé. **Client:** NBIA (New Bangkok International Airport). **Completion:** 2006. **Ecological aspects:** water energy; insulation Low-E glazing; glass air conditioning skin; three-layer translucent membrane; ventilation engineering.

↑ | **Terminal**
↓ | **Section**

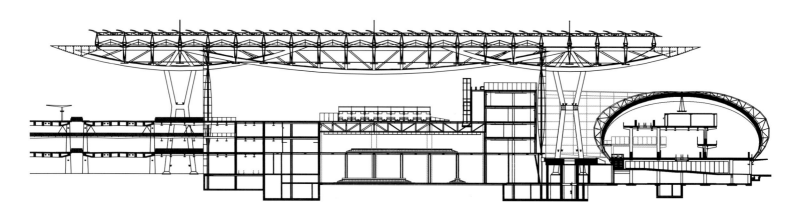

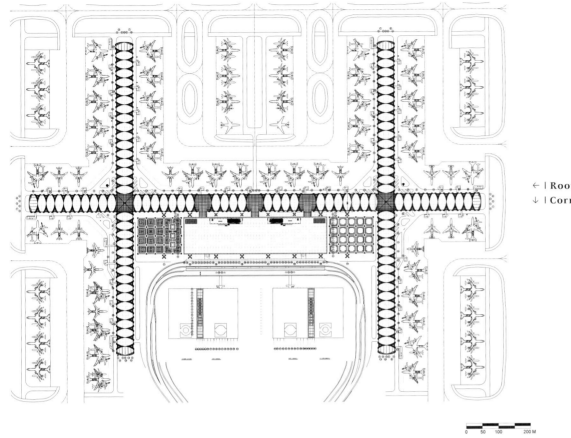

← | Roof plan
↓ | Corridor

ATP Architects and
Engineers

↑ | **Front elevation**
→ | **Entrance area**

Atrio Shopping Center
Villach

The theme behind this shopping center is its location on the border of three nations: Austria, Italy and Slovenia, which in addition to fulfilling its motto of "shopping without borders," also commits it to bridging cultural gaps. The oversized red entry frame with a protruding, steel lattice canopy sculpture takes up almost the entire southern façade. Thermal insulation is achieved using black plates clad with perforated aluminum sheeting. The building stands on top of 800 stakes, 652 of which act as heat exchangers. Water circulates in the pillars reaching 60 to 70 meters in depth, which brings geothermal energy into the center to be used to heat or cool the interior.

PROJECT FACTS

Address: Kärtner Straße 34, 9500 Villach, Austria. **Landscape architect:** GEOS Klagenfurt. **Client:** SES Spar Österreichische Warenhandels-AG. **Completion:** 2007. **Ecological aspects:** geothermal energy; 30% renewable energy. **Certificates/standards:** ReSource Award Supporting Sustainable Development 2008, TRIGOS CSR/Ecology Award 2008, Energy Globe Award 2007.

↑ | **Main entrance** at night
← | **Site plan with basement**
↓ | **Ground floor plan**

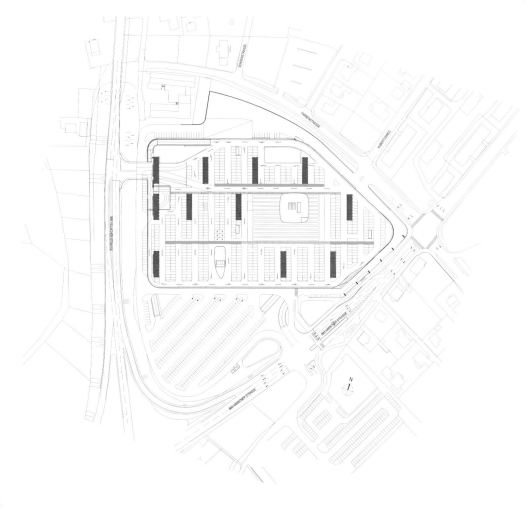

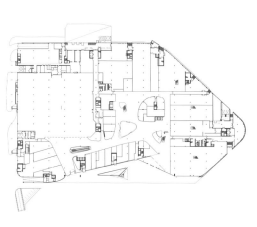

← | Terrace
↓ | Plaza

Henning Larsen Architects

↑ | **General view** from the harbor basin
→ | **Courtyard**

Ericusspitze

Hamburg

In order to create hierarchy and openness on the site as well as to embrace the complex urban spaces that meet at the Ericusspitze, the architects have chosen a two-part composition. Each building has a significant value in relation to creating identity for the surrounding public spaces. Ericusspitze embraces an internal space with a certain urban character. It comprises an open, green outdoor area directed towards the large park. The buildings form two plazas. An arrival plaza for pedestrians, cyclists and drivers towards Brooktorkai and one for relaxation, protected against traffic and noise, in direct connection to the quay promenade towards the Ericusspitze.

PROJECT FACTS

Address: Ericusspitze, 20457 Hamburg, Germany. **Planning partner:** Höhler+Partner. **Cybernetics:** DS-Plan.
MEP engineer: ISR-Ingenieurbüro Schlegel & Reußwig. **Landscape architect:** WES Landschaftsplaner.
Client: ABG/Robert Vogel. **Completion:** 2010. **Ecological aspects:** solar energy; heat exchanger, pumps,
recovery; thermoactive building systems; transmission heat loss $U < 0.26$ W/m²K (walls); airtightness
$n50 = 4$ 1/h; rainwater reuse. **Degree of sealing:** 44 %. **Certificates / standards:** low energy building.

↑ | Interior view
↓ | Ground floor plan

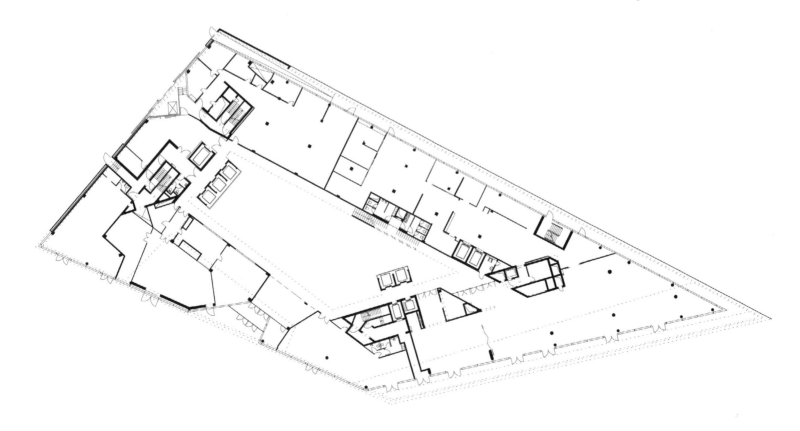

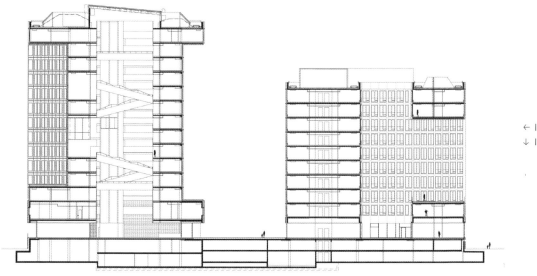

← | Sections
↓ | Staircase

Gould Evans,
Lord, Aeck & Sargent

↑ | **North-west view,** corner and façade
↗ | **South-west view**
→ | **North-east view,** corner at dusk

The Biodesign Institute at Arizona State University

Tempe

The Biodesign Institute is a bio-research facility, envisioned as both a science facility and a global demonstration of ecological laboratory design. Interdisciplinary research is the core of the Institute's strategy, and also serves as the inspiration for the building's design to enhance the values and culture of the Institute. The design locates the spaces around an open atrium that connects people visually, vertically and horizontally. The Institute incorporates a range of green design features ranging from site / urban planning to interior finishes. Adjacent to the Institute is the Bioswale Garden, made up of desert plantlife, irrigated by collected condensation and rainwater runoff.

Address: 1001 S. McAllister Avenue, Tempe, AZ 85287, USA. **MEP engineer:** Newcomb & Boyd. **Client:** Arizona State University. **Completion:** 2005. **Ecological aspects:** solar energy, variable-volume exhaust system (to minimize energy in lab ventilation); photovoltaics; high-efficiency insulation glazing; rainwater reuse; complete building automation. **Certificates/standards:** LEED Gold (building A), LEED Platinum (building B).

↑ | **Louvre detail**
↙ | **First floor plan,** building A

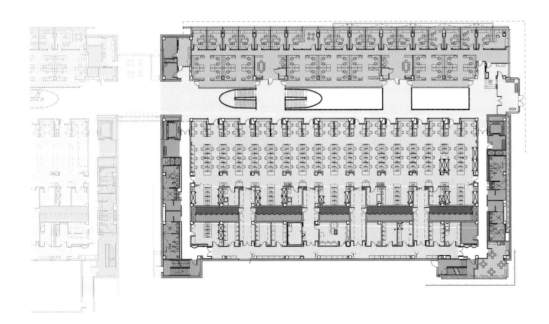

← | **Interior view atrium**
↙ | **North façade,** detail

GKK+Architekten / Dr. Oliver
Kühn, Prof. Swantje Kühn
CBP Technische Ausrüstung
GmbH / Christian Dietl

↑ | **Atrium**
→ | **Areal view**

New Headquarters for Süddeutscher Verlag
Munich

This office tower will be one of the first buildings in Germany of its type to receive the LEED Gold certification, resulting from an intelligent energy concept combined with natural ventilation, an intelligent double skin façade system and decentralized air handling units. Echoing the color coding of the newspaper production, all surfaces throughout the building are either black, white or silver. The only exception is the large two-storyed cafeteria designed in cooperation with the artist Tobias Rehberger. In contrast to the general design this area appears in bright colors with wooden flooring and a felt ceiling.

Address: Hultschiner Straße 8, 81677 Munich, Germany. **MEP engineer:** CBP Technische Ausrüstung GmbH. **Client:** SV-Hochhaus Hultschiner Straße GmbH & Co. Vermietungs-KG. **Completion:** 2008. **Ecological aspects:** geothermal energy; heat exchanger, district heating; thermoactive building systems; transmission heat loss U=1.01 W/m²K; insulation glazing U=1.1 W/m²K; rainwater reuse; building automation. **Degree of sealing:** 20%. **Certificates / standards:** EnEV, LEED Gold (candidate).

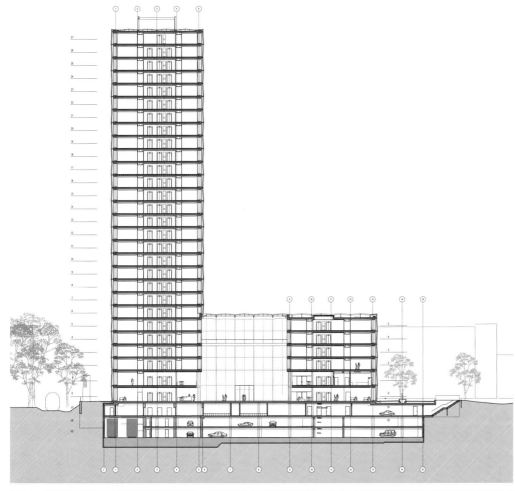

←← | Sky Lounge
← | Section
↓ | Cafeteria

GATERMANN + SCHOSSIG

↑ | **Exterior view**
→ | **Atrium**

Capricornhaus
Düsseldorf

The i-module façade conceived by the architects for this building located in an area of high acoustic pollution contains all the necessary technology for individually controlling the climate of each workspace. The modules are equipped with their own systems for cooling, heating, ventilation and heat recovery. In addition, illumination, sound insulation and room acoustic elements are integrated into the façade panels. The elimination of traditional technical areas by the decentralized i-module concept brings a high level of freedom to interior planning. Transparent and closed glass elements balance each other out, optimizing the rate of heat entry and cooling.

PROJECT FACTS

Address: Holzstraße 6, 40219 Düsseldorf, Germany. **Cybernetics:** Syscontrol GmbH. **MEP engineer:** HIT Huber Ingenieurtechnik GmbH. **Client:** Capricorn Development GmbH & Co.KG. **Completion:** 2006. **Ecological aspects:** geothermal energy; 80% renewable energy; solar heat; heat reservoir, exchanger, pumps, recovery; thermoactive building systems; transmission heat loss U=1.01 W/m²K; ventilation engineering; complete automation; 55% covered with greenery. **Certificates/standards:** low energy building.

↑ | **Offices**
← | **Cafeteria**

← | **Interior view,** trader desks
↓ | **Floor plan**

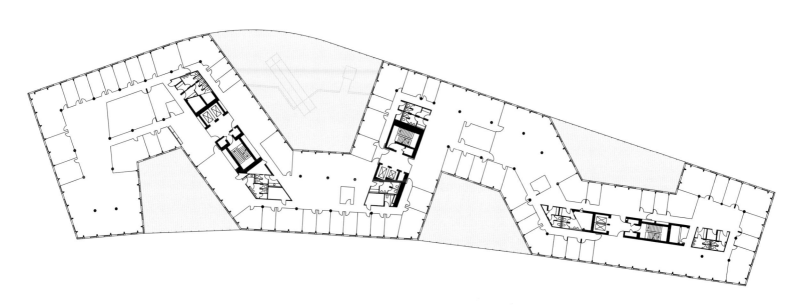

Lehrer + Gangi
Design + Build

↑ | **Side elevation**
→ | **Roof,** photovoltaic installation

Water + Life Museum
Hemet

The building links the themes of Southern California's water infrastructure and the evolution of life, explored by the sister museums. The architectural idea was derived from the great history of the Metropolitan Water District's monumental architecture and was built to achieve LEED Platinum certification, incorporating a range of efficient design features ranging from dual-flush toilets to broad expanses of solar panels. The buildings' rooftop photovoltaic installation has a 540-kilowatt solar-power system, and generates energy for 47% of the museum campus. The interior lighting design includes a network of electronic sensing devices and timers that optimize daylight recovery.

PROJECT FACTS

Address: 2325/2345 Searl Parkway, Hemet, CA 92546, USA. **Client:** The Center for Water Education and Western Center for Archaeology and Paleontology. **MEP engineer:** IBE Consulting Engineers. **Structural engineer:** Nabih Youssef & Associates. **Electrical/solar engineer:** Vector Delta Design Group. **Completion:** 2006. **Ecological aspects:** solar energy; 46% renewable energy; insulation glazing; rainwater reuse; complete building automation; ventilation engineering. **Certificates/standards:** LEED Platinum.

↑ | **Exterior view from parking lot,** land-
scaping by Mia Lehrer + Associates
← | **Corridor,** flushed with natural light

← | **Entrance area,** shaded by photovoltaic
installation on the roof
↓ | **Sustainability diagram**

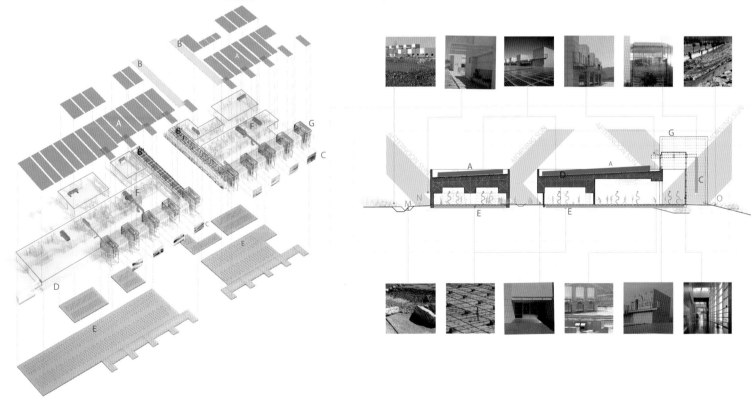

A PHOTOVOLTAICS+INSULATION
B PHOTOVOLTAICS+SHADING DEVICE
C SHADING DEVICE

D DISTANCE BETWEEN PV AND ROOF
E RADIANT HEATING + COOLING
F MINIMAL FORCED AIR UNITS
G INSULATION

H REFLECTED SUN LIGHT
I DAYLIGHT

K AWNINGS
L SUN SHADING
M IRRIGATION REDUCTION

N DRIP IRRIGATION SYSTEM
O PRECIPITATION MANAGEMENT

Renzo Piano Building
Workshop

↑ | **Living roof**
→ | **Interior view,** dome-shaped roof with skylights

California Academy of Sciences
San Francisco

The building is an attempt to develop workable and sustainable public architecture. It demonstrates these goals with its living green roof, which echoes the landscape of the surrounding Golden Gate Park and acts as superior thermal insulation. Flexible, integrated spaces provide room for exhibitions inside. Radiant floor heating, heat recovery systems and high-performance glass are used to reduce heat absorption and to keep energy requirements at a minimum level. The majority of the spaces inside the building have access to daylight, diminishing the need of artificial lighting. Photo sensors are implemented to dim artificial lighting in response to daylight penetration.

PROJECT FACTS

Address: 55 Music Concourse Drive, San Francisco, CA 94118, USA. **Structural engineers:** Ove Arup & Partners. **Planning partner:** Stantec Architecture. **Civil engineers:** Rutherford & Chekene. **Landscaping:** SWA Group. **Living roof:** Rana Creek. **Aquarium life support systems:** PBS&J. **Exhibits:** Thinc Design, Cinnabar, Visual-Acuity. **Client:** California Academy of Sciences. **Completion:** 2008. **Ecological aspects:** heat reservoir; recycled old Academy, rainwater reuse; ventilation engineering. **Degree of sealing:** 31%.

↑ | **Front view,** entrance area
↓ | **Sketch,** climatic concept

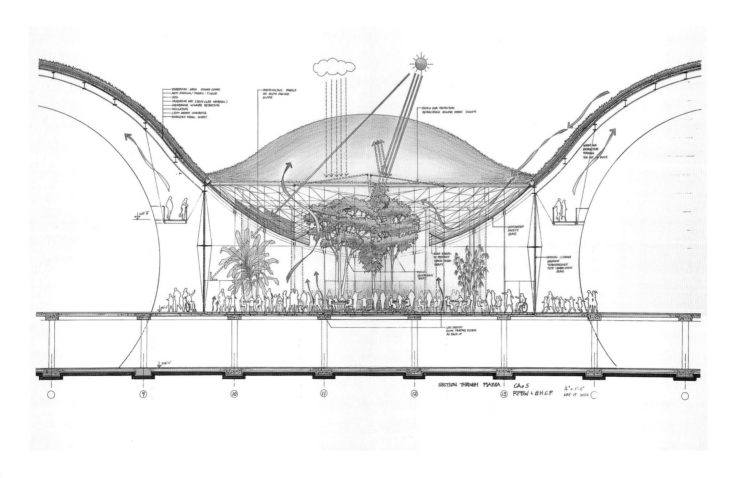

↖ | Roof
← | Entrance area

Foreign Office Architects /
Farshid Moussavi,
Alejandro Zaera-Polo

↑ | **Restaurant**
↗ | **Central square**
→ | **Aerial view**

Şhopping Square Meydan – Ümraniye

Retail complex and multiplex, Istanbul

The development is not only a proficient retail complex, but rather an urban center for future development of one of the fastest growing areas in Istanbul. The building anticipates its subsequent integration into a dense inner city context through its geometry and circulation strategy, aiming to formulate an alternative prototype to the usual city outskirt retail box development. The provision of underground car parking is a major part of this strategy, liberating substantial amounts of ground floor space to be used for landscaped areas and a new urban square as the core of the scheme. All roofs are covered with extensive vegetation and skylights, providing daylight and ventilation for the inner spaces.

PROJECT FACTS

Address: Çakmak Mh. Metro Group Sok. No. 243, Ümraniye Meydan, Istanbul, Turkey. **Structural engineer:** Adams Kara Taylor. **Landscape architect:** GTL – Güchtel Triebswetter Landschaftsarchitekten. **Client:** METRO Group Asset Management. **Completion:** 2007. **Ecological aspects:** geothermal energy; ventilation engineering; 30,000 m² covered with greenery; geothermal system reduces 350 tons CO_2/year.

↑ | **Cinema** at night
← | **Central square**

← | Inside the mall
↓ | Site masterplan

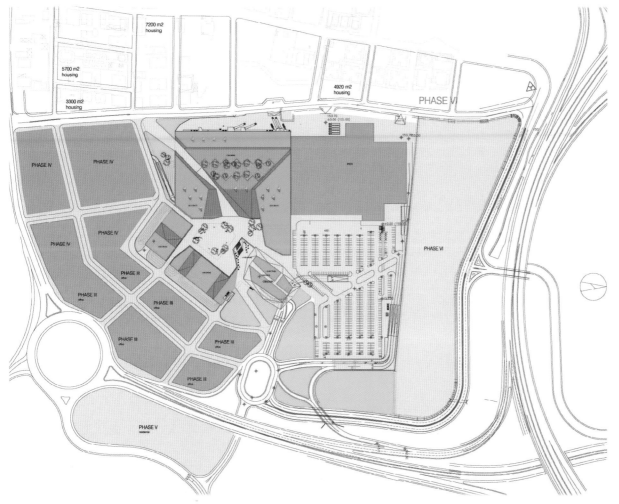

Foster + Partners

↑ | **Worm's-eye view**
→ | **Elevation**

Hearst Tower

New York City

The Hearst Tower is the first office building in New York City recognized by the U.S. Green Building Council for high environmental performance on both its exterior and interior. Key features are a Low-E glass envelope, light sensors to control the use of artificial light based on availability of natural light, activity level sensors that control both lights and computers, high efficiency HVAC systems (Heating Ventilation Air Conditioning), and the use of outside make-up air for cooling and ventilation. The building also employs pioneer technologies to conserve water. Rainwater is collected on the roof, reducing the amount of water dumped into the sewer system. It is expected that the captured rain will produce about half of the water needs, while also serving to humidify and chill the atrium.

PROJECT FACTS

Address: 224 West, 57th Street/8th Avenue, New York City, NY 10019, USA. **Planning partner:** Adamson Associates. **Original building:** Joseph Urban, 1928. **Client:** Hearst Corporation. **Completion:** 2006. **Ecological aspects:** recycled steel (85%); rainwater reuse; light sensors for saving electrical light; ventilation engineering; sustainable because of saving steel. **Certificates/standards:** LEED Gold.

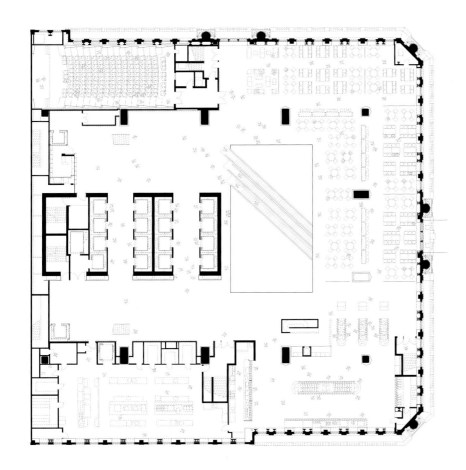

←←| **Detail façade**
← | **Floor plan**
↓ | **Section**

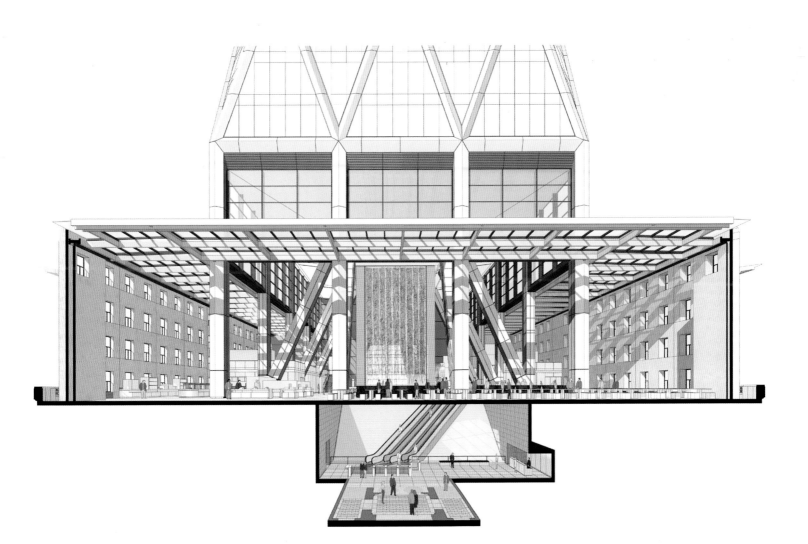

Dissing + Weitling
arkitektfirma

↑ | **The news studio**
→ | **Solar panels,** view from the atrium

Danish Broadcasting
Media House

Copenhagen

Sustainable technologies are highly integrated with the overall design strategy of the new home to Denmark's national broadcasting corporation. The eco-friendly design focuses on integrated solutions. These include a double-façade which allows natural ventilation and night cooling, and a ground water cooling system, fed in turn by the solar cell louver array on the roof, where rainwater is collected for secondary usage. The state-of-the-art multi-functional double façade system and award-winning solar panel installation demonstrate an environmental consciousness, contributing technically as well as aesthetically to the overall architectural expression of the Media House.

PROJECT FACTS

Address: Ørestads Boulevard 19, 2300 Copenhagen, Denmark. **MEP engineer:** NIRAS, ARUP. **Client:** Danish Broadcasting Corporation. **Completion:** 2006. **Ecological aspects:** solar, geothermal energy; solar heat; ground water cooling system; glass air conditioning skin; rainwater reuse; ventilation engineering. **Degree of sealing:** 100%.

↑ | **Double-skin façades,** east view
← | **Site plan**

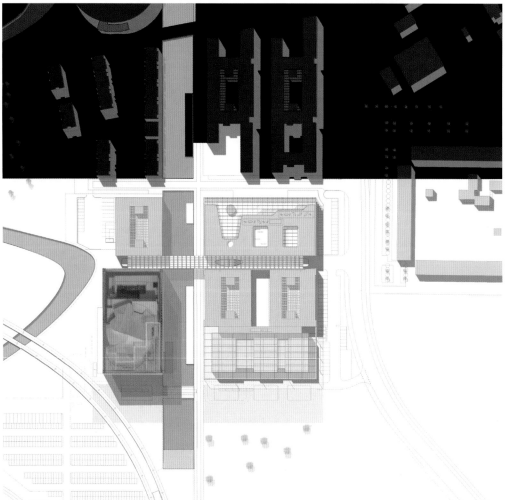

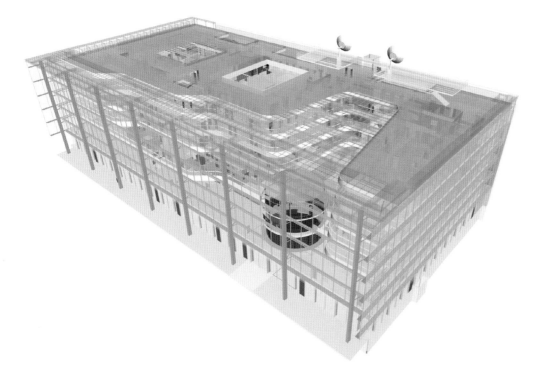

← | 3-D rendering
↓ | **Interior view**, atrium

Extra Large

↑ | **Bird's-eye view,** solar panels on every roof
→ | **View of the housing development**

Schlierberg Solar Settlement
Freiburg

Freiburg's Vauban district was built on former inner city military grounds, and its eastern section became the Solar settlement. It includes 50 row homes as well as the Sun Ship commercial building with nine penthouse units – with a gross living space of 1,160 square meters, and 5,000 square meters of commercial/office space. All buildings were erected using Energy-plus construction methods: in an annual cycle, they produce more energy than what they use. In addition to energy efficiency, large area photovoltaic collectors are decisive, reaching a peak of production at 445 kilowatts and a total production of about 420,000 kilowatt hours.

PROJECT FACTS

Address: Merzhauser Straße 177, 79100 Freiburg, Germany. **Client:** Solarsiedlung GmbH. **Completion:** 2004. **Ecological aspects:** solar panels; ventilation with heat recovery; thermoactive building systems (phase changing material); vacuum insulation; central pellets cogeneration unit; triple glazed windows (infrared layered). **Certificates/standards:** energy-plus house.

↑ | **North-east view,** vivid colors create a friendly atmosphere
← | **Plans,** different house types found in the housing development

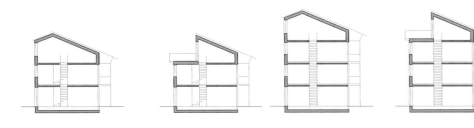

← | Site plan
↓ | South-west view

X Architects,
SMAQ – architecture
urbanism research

↑ | **The active edge** between the landscape and
the built form

XERITOWN

Dubailand

The project is a 590,000 square meter sustainable mixed use development in one of the
fastest growing cities of the world: Dubai. Unlike most projects in Dubai, which often
consider their site as a tabula rasa, Xeritown takes the desert and local climate as a context
within which the urban form emerges by working with the natural environment instead of
against it. The project incorporates several passive measures like sun and wind-based orientation, compacted urban footprint and a rugged skyline in conjunction with active strategies like LED street lighting, district cooling, gray water recycling and renewable energy
generation to reduce overall energy demand and create a socially vibrant urban setting.

PROJECT FACTS
Address: Plot No. B33-B, Bawadi Site, Dubailand, Dubai, U.A.E. **MEP engineer:** Buro Happold. **Landscape architect:** Johannes Grothaus. **Client:** INJAZ LLC. **Completion:** 2012. **Ecological aspects:** solar, wind, geothermal energy; solar heat; earth pipes for air conditioning; insulation glazing will incorporate solar protective coatings; rainwater reuse; ventilation engineering. **Degree of sealing:** 50%. **Certificates/standards:** various LEED certificates.

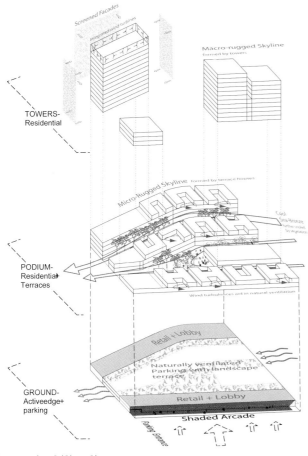

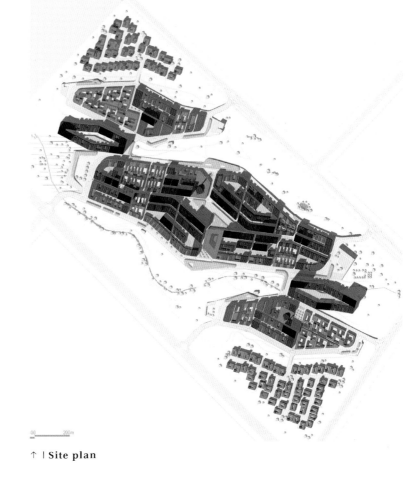

↑ | **Sustainability diagram**
↓ | **Aerial view** of the master plan

↑ | **Site plan**

↑ | **View from garden**
↗ | **View from backyard**
→ | **Façades**

Solar Standard

Moscow

This urban development is located in Moscow and encompasses residential spaces for 2,000 to 3,000 inhabitants with embedded recreatinol areas. The residential area is organized mainly in single-house units utilizing environmentally friendly construction. The houses are planned as hypermodern compositions in various sizes and are all oriented to the south. Sustainability was gained with the choice of recycled and recyclable materials as well as by optimizing the energy characteristics of both the building structure and technical configuration. Furthermore, the goal of carbon emissions reduction was pursued by creating a path system which allows the whole area to be explored by foot.

PROJECT FACTS

Address: Kotovo, Moscow, Russia. **Client:** RI GROUP. **Completion:** ongoing. **Ecological aspects:** solar, wind energy; 80% renewable energy; solar heat; heat reservoir, exchanger, recovery; thermoactive building systems; rainwater reuse; ventilation engineering; passive solar energy; 150,000 m² covered with greenery. **Degree of sealing:** 12%. **Certificates/standards:** passive energy building.

↑ | **Trails** for walking by foot
↙ | **Floor plan**
↓ | **Roof light**

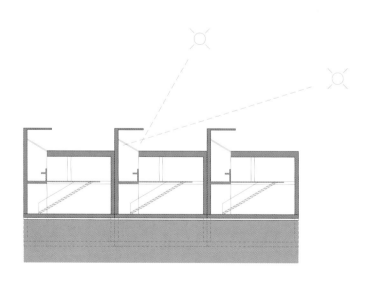

← | **Interior view**, roof lights
↙ | **Site plan**

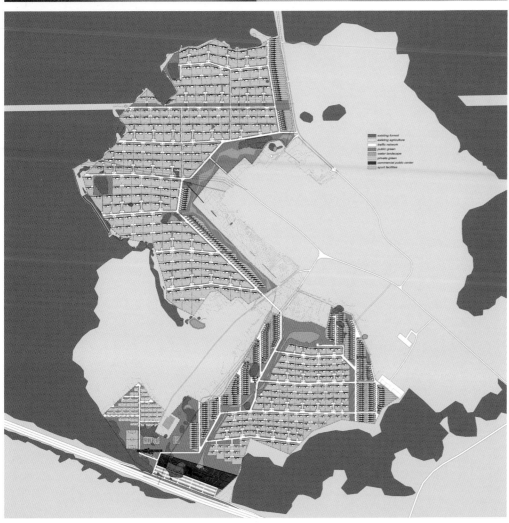

Michael Sorkin Studio

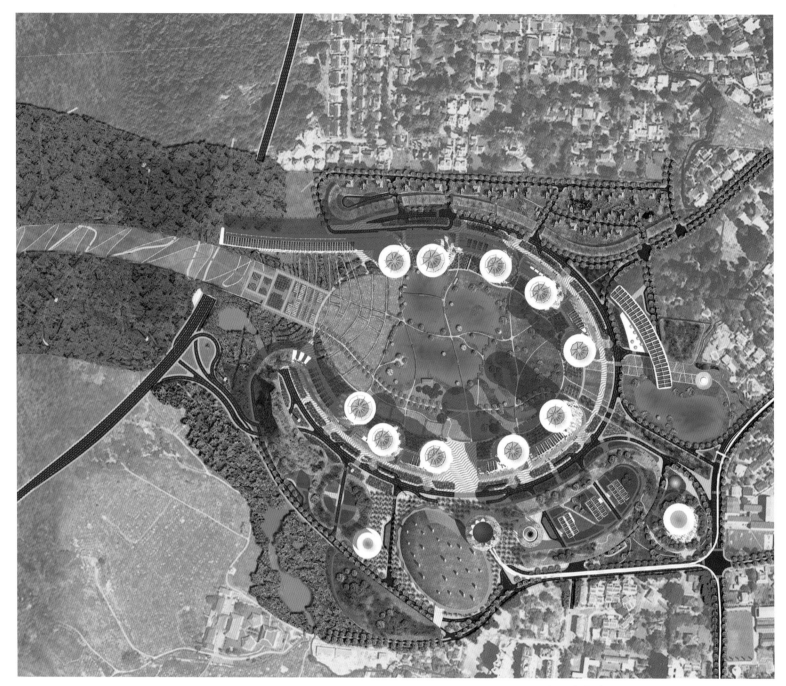

↑ | **Aerial view**

Penang Peaks

Penang

The beautiful site of the Penang Turf Club is a blessing and a challenge at the same time. Any development of the area has to be balanced – maintaining the flow of green space while revealing the potential of the site. Therefore, the project is organized around a park intended as an amenity for the city as a whole and is linked to Penang Hill via a bridge over the Penang Outer Ring Road. Residential buildings frame the boundaries of the park. It was taken care that the architecture of the place is sustainable in appearance as well as operation. The scheme includes an elaborate system for rainwater and run-off harvesting, photovoltaic plants and solar water heaters, allowing the mix-used project to function "off the grid."

PROJECT FACTS **Address:** Penang, Malaysia. **Client:** Equine Properties. **Completion:** ongoing. **Ecological aspects:** solar energy; passive heating/cooling; rainwater reuse; on-site waste. **Certificates/standards:** low energy building.

↑ | **Environmental diagram**
↓ | **Elevation**

↑ | **Equine tower**

↑ | **Aerial view**

Treasure Island Master Plan

San Francisco

Bold moves set the framework for the redevelopment of Treasure Island – a former Navy base located two miles across the bay from downtown San Francisco. The plan envisions one commercial district and four residential neighborhoods, which would house ten thousand residents. A complex and thoroughly articulated urban design and architectural plan establishes relationships between buildings, public open space, transportation, views, and natural forces, creating a compact, transit-oriented, pedestrian-friendly community with a commitment to sustainability. Great care was taken in planning a public transport system which discourages car use while enabling a high level of individual mobility.

PROJECT FACTS

Address: San Francisco, CA, USA. **Master planning/urban design:** Skidmore, Owings & Merrill, LLP; SMWM, CMG Overall Conceptual. **Associated architects:** SMWM, BCV, Hornberger Worstell. **Landscape architecture:** CMG with Tom Leader. **Sustainable design:** ARUP Civil. **Engineering and transportation:** Korve, ARUP, Concept Marine Associates. **Geotechnical design:** Treadwell & Rollo, Engeo. **Client:** Treasure Island Community Development, LLC. **Completion:** ongoing.

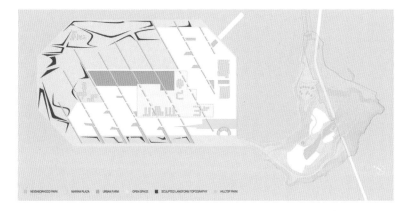

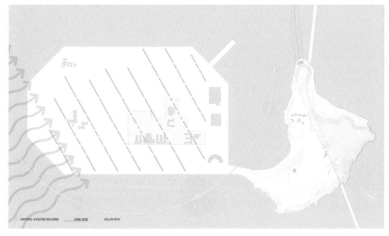

↑ | **Open space,** wind rows
↓ | **Exterior view**

↑ | **Plan,** sun and wind

JDS – Julien de Smedt
architects

↑ | Façade
↗ | Interior
→ | Plaza

Shenzhen Logistic City
Shenzhen

The architect's task was to design a new urban quarter in Shenzhen, which was to create five million square meters of usable space and be 1,111 meters tall. It turned out that the main task in creating a project in these dimensions was not about fitting the surfaces onto the site, but achieving a socially and logistically functioning vertical city. In order to avoid building merely a skyscraper with levels which are only connected by elevators, the architects wanted to re-introduce the natural element of a mountainous site. Following this basic concept, a design rich in greenery and with an airy feel, and which has undulating paths and connects the different levels of this green building was created.

PROJECT FACTS

Address: Shenzhen, Guangdong 518000, China. **Client:** City of Shenzhen. **Completion:** ongoing.
Ecological aspects: ventilation and climatization via integrated landscaped areas, high-rise character
of the building reduces degree of soil sealing, further aspects to be specified.

↑ | **Site plan**
← | **Façade,** detail

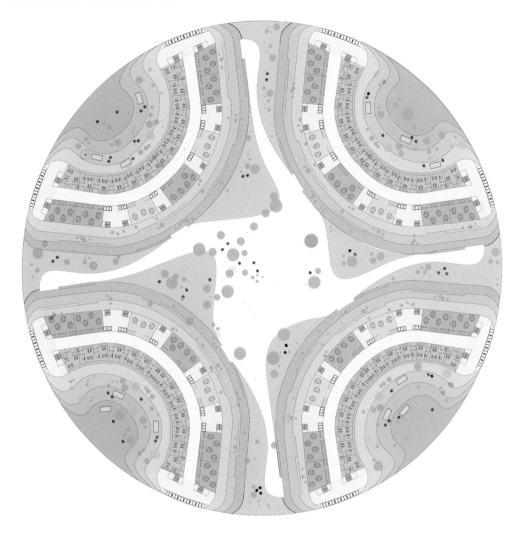

← | **Floor plan**
↙ | **Distance view** of the building

BIG – Bjarke Ingels Group

↑ | Terraced housing
↗ | Aerial view
→ | View from canal side

Mountain Dwellings
Copenhagen

This housing project is an attempt to combine the splendors of suburban living with the social density of an urban area. In order to create large spaces for parking and living and to fulfill the different requirements of these spaces, a connection between the two functions was made. The parking area with access to the street became the base on which the living spaces in the form of terraced housing were placed. All 80 apartments have roof gardens that are maintained by a huge watering system and allow high levels of sunlight penetration. The north and west façades are covered by perforated aluminum plates, which let air and light into the parking area, helping to reduce energy consumption.

PROJECT FACTS

Address: Orestads Bulevard 55, 2300, Copenhagen, Denmark. **Planning partner:** JDS architects. **Structural engineer:** Moe & Brødsgaard and Frode Madsen engineers. **Artist:** Victor Ash. **Landscape architect:** SLA. **Client:** Høpfner A/S, Danish Oil Company A/S. **Completion:** 2008. **Ecological aspects:** artificial water irrigation system; insulation glazing.

↑ | **Top apartments**
↓ | **West elevation**

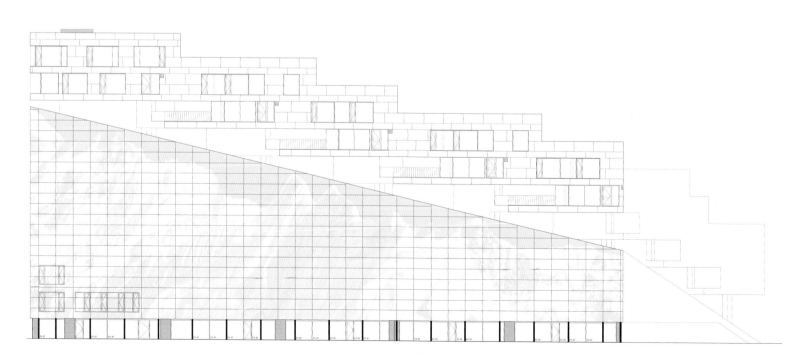

← | Detail backside
↓ | Parking area

↑ | **Aerial view**

Nanao Resort

Su-ao Town

The masterplan of the resort is carved around a man-made lake as a figural environmental etching of an Atayal aborigine tattoo on the vast land. The buildings, of traditional aboriginal stone construction, perch on the water's edge like sculptural rock formations. The main building traces the hilly topography with its sinewy, undulating form to become the eastern contour of the lake. The Water Villa is designed as an entire island, with spaces sculpted from within the landmass and overhanging stone eaves that grow into the island's edge. The Eco-pods, scattered throughout the indigenous eucalyptus forest, are particular camping structures with an upward spiraling plan that pivots around a central fireplace.

PROJECT FACTS

Address: 92, Hai-an Rd.m Su-ao Town, Yilan County, Taiwan (R.O.C.). **Client:** Ambassador Hotel. **Completion:** 2011. **Ecological aspects:** low-slung stone clad massing, earth berm structure, generous overhang solar shading; heat pumps; low solar gain, active natural ventilation, sheltered patios; recycled local stone; insulation glazing Low-E double pane/UV film; rainwater reuse; ventilation engineering. **Degree of sealing:** 2%. **Certificates/standards:** low energy building.

↑ | **Water Villa,** a villa carved from an island

↓ | **View of the lake**

↑ | **Eco-pods** scattered in the eucalyptus forest

↑ | **Façade**
→ | **Exterior view** during night

Generali Tower

Paris

Sustainability is at the heart of the architectural concept of the Generali Tower. The building's innovative structure and envelope, as well as the choice of its technical and mechanical equipment (opening windows, suspended gardens at all levels) enhance the user's comfort while reducing energy consumption. Production of renewable energy has also been incorporated in the tower's design: vertical axis wind turbines and solar panels are located in the towers central spire, photovoltaic cells line the inside of the peaks, adding a unique silhouette to the La Défense skyline. Encompassing 90,000 square meters of gross floor area, the tower will house various facilities including an auditorium, multiple restaurants and a child care center.

PROJECT FACTS

Address: La Défense, Paris, France. **MEP engineer:** IOSIS. **Client:** Generali Immobilier Gestion. **Completion:** 2013. **Ecological aspects:** solar, wind energy; solar heat, insulation glazing (solar factor 27%, light transmission 50%); rainwater reuse; complete building automation; ventilation engineering, natural ventilation due to operable panels. **Certificates/standards:** low energy building, HQE, BREEAM.

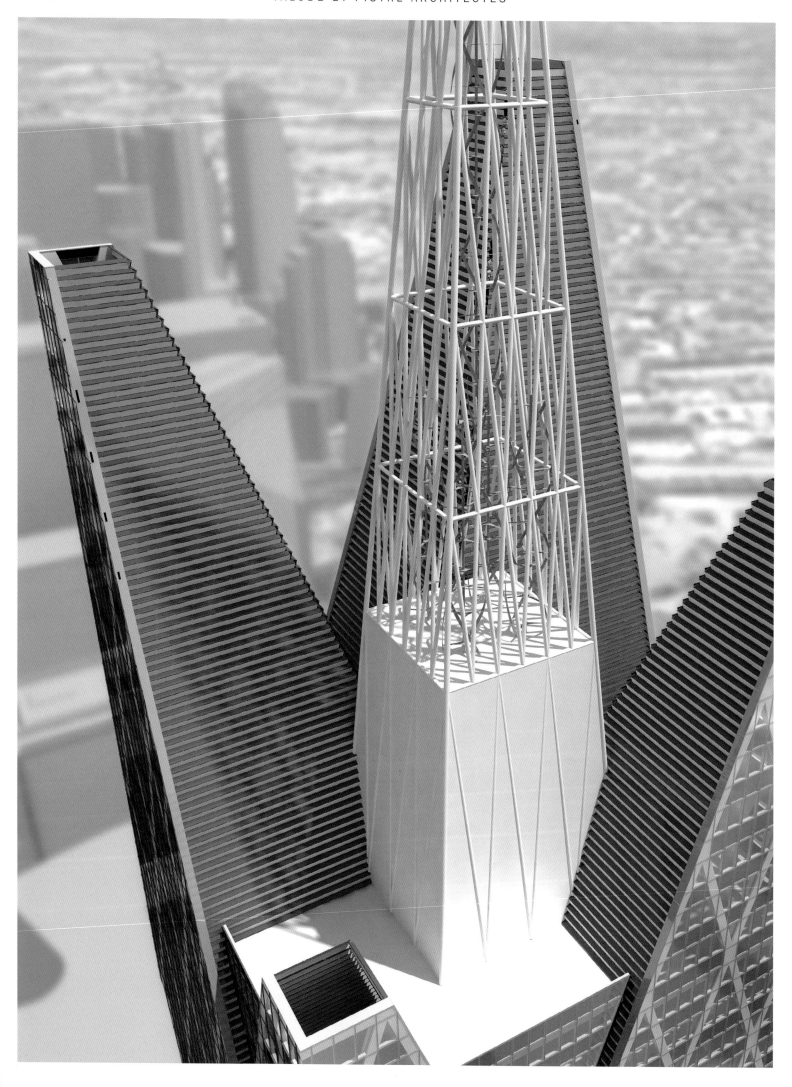

←← | **Central spire and peaks** with vertical axis wind turbines, photovoltaic cells and solar panels
← | **Exterior garden**
↓ | **Interior view**

↑ | **General view**

Ciudad del Medio Ambiente

Santomera

The competition envisions the recovery of a stone quarry in the Murcia region. The project is generating environmental recovery of high quality and creates a series of spaces to house activities dedicated to profound environmental themes: a true city of ecology. The goal of the proposal is to offer a product which awakes interest in the majority of population belonging to various social groups, as well as to achieve recognition of Murcia's Environmental City.

PROJECT FACTS **Address:** 30140 Santomera, Spain. **Forest engineer:** Victor Manuel Castillo Sánchez. **Structural engineer:** Julián Pérez Castillo. **Client:** Dirección General de Medio Natural de la Región de Murcia. **Completion:** 2011. **Ecological aspects:** solar, wind energy; thermoactive building systems; recycled resilient rubber flooring, recycled cork; insulation glazing 5 cm glass fiber; rainwater reuse; ventilation engineering; 500 m² covered with green. **Degree of sealing:** 1.6 %. **Certificates/standards:** zero energy building.

↑ | **View from lake side**
↓ | **View of pavilions**

↑ | **General plan**

↑ | **Entrance area**
→ | **Shopping arcade**

Masdar Development

Abu Dhabi

Masdar development combines traditional principles of a walled city with new technologies to achieve a carbon neutral, zero waste community that responds to the urban identity of Abu Dhabi. It will be linked to the existing city transport infrastructure and to the surrounding communities by a network of new rail and public transport routes. In order to avoid carbon emissions, the city will be car-free, employing instead a personalized transport system, serving a maximum radius of 200 meters. With carefully planned future expansion, the surrounding land will contain photovoltaic farms, research fields and plantations to achieve an entirely self-sustaining city.

PROJECT FACTS

Address: Abu Dhabi, United Arab Emirates. **Planning partner:** Cyril Sweet Limited, W.S.P Transsolar, ETA, Gustafson Porter, ETA., Energy, Ernst and Young, Flack + Kurtz, Systematica, Transsolar. **Client:** Masdar-Abu Dhabi Future Energy Company, Mubadala Development Company. **Completion:** 2023. **Ecological aspects:** solar, wind energy; photovoltaic plant system; avoiding low density sprawl; car-free transport system for carbon neutral city. **Certificates/standards:** zero energy city.

↑ | Arcade
← | Interior view

← | **Master plan**
↓ | **Interior view** at night

Silvio Rech, Lesley Carstens
Architects and Interior
Architects

↑ | **Aerial view**
↗ | **Villa,** bird's-eye view
→ | **Bedroom**

North Island
Seychelles

North Island was planned as a "Noah's Ark project" and involved the restoration of an entire island from its damaged state brought on by commercial exploitation that began in 1826. The island had been used as a plantation for growing fruits and spices and, later, producing copra – oil pressed from coconut flesh. Cultivation and replanting of native plants as well as removal of alien species was a major part of the project. Several rental villas handcrafted form local wood and stone were erected. The proceeds are used to bankroll the renaturalization project. The interplay of architecture, landscape architecture and interior design established a new style – the "Robinson Crusoe Haute Couture."

PROJECT FACTS

Address: North Island, Seychelles. **Landscape architect:** Patrick Watson. **Interiors:** Life Interiors. **Conservation projects:** Wilderness Safaris. **Client:** North Island Co. **Completion:** 2003. **Ecological aspects:** materials reaped from the rehabilitation process; renaturalisation of the complete island with native plants. **Certificates/standards:** Indian Ocean's Leading Green Resort.

↖ | **Pool of a villa**
← | **Local vegetation** along the main pool

← | **Relaxation**
↓ | **Site plan,** main area

KEY

1   main piazza
2   main lounge
3   main bar
4   main dinning room
5   wine cellar
6   office
7   kitchen
8   library
9   dive centre office
10 dive centre
11 shop
    axis

Index

Arch

itects Index

5 Architekten AG

Landstrasse 170
5430 Wettingen (Switzerland)
T +41.56.4371055
F +41.56.4371059
info@5architekten.ch
www.5architekten.ch

→ 92

24H architecture

Hoflaan 132
3062 JM Rotterdam (The Netherlands)
T +31.10.4111000
F +31.10.2827287
info@24h.eu
www.24h.eu

→ 22

Ad hoc Arquitectos

Bename, 1
30005 Murcia (Spain)
T +34.968.274278
F +34.968.298686
info@adhocmsl.com
www.adhocmsl.com

→ 416

Allmann Sattler Wappner Architekten GmbH

Nymphenburger Straße 125
80636 Munich (Germany)
T +49.89.1399250
F +49.89.13992599
info@allmannsattlerwappner.de
www.allmannsattlerwappner.de

→ 326

Alejandro Aravena

El Comendador 1916
Providencia Santiago (Chile)
T +56.2.3547749
F +56.2.3547749
aravenamori@gmail.com
www.alejandroaravena.com

→ 146

ARCHTEAM

Namesti Svobody 9
602 00 Brno (Czech Republic)
T +420.542.213617
F +420.542.213617
archteam@archteam.cz
www.archteam.cz

→ 164

ATP Architects and Engineers

ATP-Haus, Heiliggeiststraße 16
6010 Innsbruck (Austria)
T +43.512.53700
info@atp.ag
www.atp.ag

→346

Bachman + Bachmann Architecture Office

Böckh J. Street 1
7625 Pécs (Hungary)
T +36.30.5201064
moto354@freemail.hu

→ 306

barbarela studio

Calle Mayor 19, 31
03002 Alicante (Spain)
T +34.955.203319
F +34.955.203319
info@barbarela.biz
www.barbarela.biz

→ 416

Charles Barclay Architects

74 Josephine Avenue
London SW2 2LA (United Kingdom)
T +44.20.86740037
F +44.20.86839696
cba@cbarchitects.co.uk
www.cbarchitects.co.uk

→ 62

BEHNISCH ARCHITECTS, Inc.

35 Market Street
Venice, CA 90291 (USA)
T +1.310.3999003
F +1.310.3999677
bala@behnisch.com
www.behnisch.com

BEHNISCH ARCHITEKTEN

Rotebühlstraße 163A
70197 Stuttgart (Germany)
T +49.711.607720
F +49.711.6077299
ba@behnisch.com
www.behnisch.com

bestBefore

San Andres 7 4B
30005 Murcia (Spain)
T +34.968.909864
F +34.968.909865
estudio@bestbefore.es

Bétrix & Consolascio Architekten

Seestrasse 78
8703 Erlenbach (Switzerland)
T +41.44.9109000
F +41.44.9109040
info@b-c-arch.ch
www.b-c-arch.ch

bhss – architekten GmbH / Behnisch Hermus Schinko Schumann

Erich-Zeigner-Allee 69–73
04229 Leipzig (Germany)
T +49.341.4867430
F +49.341.4867444
info@bhss-architekten.com
www.bhss-architekten.com

BIG – Bjarke Ingels Group

Nørrebrogade 66d 2.sal
2200 Copenhagen N (Denmark)
T +45.7221.7227
big@big.de
www.big.dk

Obie G. Bowman/Architect FAIA

P.O. Box 1114
Healdsburg, CA 95448 (USA)
T +1.707.4337833
F +1.707.8947733
ogb@obiebowman.com
www.obiebowman.com

Bucholz McEvoy Architects

Unit C Mountpleasant Business Centre, Upper Mountpleasant Avenue
Dublin 6 (Ireland)
T +353.1.4966340
F +353.1.4966341
info@bmcea.com
www.bmcea.com

BVN Architecture

17 York Street
Sydney, NSW 2000 (Australia)
T +61.2.8297.7200
F +61.2.8297.7299
sydney@bvn.com.au
www.bvn.com.au

Cambridge Seven Associates, Inc.

1050 Massachusetts Avenue
Cambridge, MA 02138 (USA)
T +1.617.4927000
F +1.617.4927007
joltman@c7a.com
www.c7a.com

CBP Technische Ausrüstung GmbH

Georg-Muche-Straße 1
80807 Munich (Germany)
T +49.89.286330
T +49.89.2863380
info@cbp.de
www.cbp.de

CENTOLA & ASSOCIATI

Piazza Umberto I, 2
84121 Salerno (Italy)
T +39.089.237113
F +39.089.237114
l.centola@awn.it
www.centolaassociati.it

→ 32, 244, 338

CO Architects

5055 Wilshire Blvd, 9th floor
Los Angeles, CA 90036 (USA)
T +1.323.5250500
F +1.323.5250955
inquires@coarchitects.com
www.coarchitects.com

→ 284

Jo Coenen & Co

Keizersgracht 126
1015 CW Amsterdam (The Netherlands)
T +31.20.5307010
F +31.20.5307020
jcca@jocoenen.com
www.jocoenen.com

→ 288

Croxton Collaborative Architects, PC

475 Fifth Avenue, 22nd Floor
New York City, NY 10017 (USA)
T +1.212.6831998
F +1.212.6832799
cca@croxtonarc.com
www.croxtonarc.com

→ 212, 258

Mario Cucinella Architects

Via De' Carracci, 93
40129 Bologna (Italy)
T +39.051.6313381
F +39.051.6313316
mca@mcarchitects.it
www.mcarchitects.it

→ 214

De8 Architetti

Via portico 59/61
24050 Orio al Serio (Italy)
T +39.035.530050
F +39.035.533725
info@deottostudio.com
www.deottostudio.com

→ 244

DEGW Australia

Level 5, 395 Collins Street
Melbourne, VIC 3000 (Australia)
T +61.2.92598900
F +61.2.9259.8901
swittenoom@degw.com
www.degw.com

→ 276

DeSo – Defrain Souquet Architects

10, rue des Bluets
75011 Paris (France)
T +33.55.439707
F +33.55.439706
defrain.souquet.archi@wanadoo.fr
www.deso-architecture.com

→ 60

Despang Architekten

Am Graswege 5
30169 Hanover (Germany)
T +49.511.882840
F +49.511.887985
info@despangarchitekten.de
www.despangarchitekten.de

→ 152

Rolf Disch SolarArchitektur

Merzhauser Straße 177
79100 Freiburg (Germany)
T +49.761.459440
F +49.761.4594444
info@rolfdisch.de
www.rolfdisch.de

→ 388

DISSING+WEITLING arkitektfirm

Dronningensgade 68
1420 Copenhagen (Denmark)
T +45.3283.5000
F +45.3283.5100
email@dw.dk
www.dw.dk

→ 382

Döll – Atelier voor Bouwkunst

Haringvliet 100
3011 TH Rotterdam (The Netherlands)
T +31.10.2718200
F +31.10.2718222
mail@dollab.nl
www.dollab.nl

→ 118

driendl architects

Mariahilferstraße 9
1060 Vienna (Austria)
T +43.1.5851868
F +43.1.5851869
architekt@driendl.at
www.driendl.at

→ 394

Ehrich + Vogel Architekten

Ateliergebäude Kölner Straße 59
40211 Düsseldorf (Germany)
T +49.211.17520740
F +49.211.175207410
architektur@ehrich-vogel.de
www.ehrich-vogel.de

→ 310

ENOTA

Poljanska cesta 6
1000 Ljubljana (Slovenia)
T +386.1.4386740
F +386.1.4386745
enota@enota.si
www.enota.si

→ 314

FAR frohn&rojas

Condominio Los Cántaros, Parcela 8, Comuna Lampa
Santiago RM (Chile)
T +56.2.7331691
F +56.2.7331691
santiago@f-a-r.net
www.f-a-r.net

→ 104

Foreign Office Architects

55 Curtain Road
London EC2A 3PT (United Kingdom)
T +44.207.0339800
F +44.207.0339801
london@f-o-a.net
www.f-o-a.net

→ 374

Foster + Partners

Riverside, 22 Hester Road
London SW11 4AN (United Kingdom)
T +44.20.77380455
F +44.20.77381107
enquiries@fosterandpartners.com
www.fosterandpartners.com

→ 378, 418

Massimiliano e Doriana Fuksas

Piazza del Monte di Pietà, 30
00186 Rome (Italy)
T +39.06.68807871
F +39.06.68807872
office@fuksas.it
www.fuksas.it

→ 318

FXFOWLE ARCHITECTS, LLP

22 West 19 Street
New York City, NY 10011 (USA)
T +1.212.6271700
www.fxfowle.com

→ 148, 362

GATERMANN + SCHOSSIG

Richartzstraße 10
50667 Cologne (Germany)
T +49.221.9258210
F +49.221.92582170
info@gatermann-schossig.de
www.gatermann-schossig.de

→ 148, 362

Esterbrogade 69D
1620 Copenhagen (Denmark)
T +45.3378.1010
F +45.3378.1029
office@jdsarchitects.com
www.jdsarchitects.com

→ 402

JOURDA Architectes Paris

4, cité Paradis
75010 Paris (France)
T +33.155.288220
F +33.155.228518
archi@jourda-architectes.com
www.jourda-architectes.com

→ 226

Jourdan & Müller PAS

Gräfstraße 79
60486 Frankfurt / Main (Germany)
T +49.69.9708180
F +49.69.97081811
mail@jourdan-mueller.de
www.jourdan-mueller.de

→ 134

Kaden Klingbeil Architekten

Esmarchstraße 3
10407 Berlin (Germany)
T +49.30.48624662
F +49.30.48624661
info@kaden-klingbeil.de
www.kaden-klingbeil.de

→ 246

Hermann Kaufmann ZT GmbH

Sportplatzweg 5
6858 Schwarzach (Austria)
T +43.5572.58174
F +43.5572.58013
office@hermann-kaufmann.at
www.hermann-kaufmann.at

→ 236, 272

Kaundbe Architekten

Egertastrasse 6
9490 Vaduz (Liechtenstein)
T +423.239.6660
F +423.239.6669
architekten@k-b.li
www.k-b.li

→ 82

Kistelegdi Architecture Office

Bagoly Dülö 8
7635 Pécs (Hungary)
T +36.30.5172617
kistelegdis@gmail.com

→266, 306

Kjellgren Kaminsky Architecture AB

Ekmansgatan 3
411 32 Gothenburg (Sweden)
T +46.31.7612001
F +46.31.182104
info@kjellgrenkaminsky.se
www.kjellgrenkaminsky.se

→ 48

Kossmann.dejong

De Ruyterkade 107
1011 AB Amsterdam (The Netherlands)
T +31.20.4208890
F +31.20.6208368
info@kossmanndejong.nl
www.kossmanndejong.nl

→ 118

Kresing Architekten

Lingener Straße 12
48155 Münster (Germany)
T +49.251.987780
F +49.251.9877810
info@kresing.de
www.kresing.de

→ 190

The Kubala Washatko Architects, Inc.

W61 N617 Mequon Avenue
Cedarburg, WI 53012 (USA)
T +1.262.3776039
F +1.262.3772954
info@tkwa.com
www.tkwa.com

→ 122

ARCHITECTS INDEX

Peter Kuczia

Osningstraße 34
49082 Osnabrück (Germany)
T +49.163.9295050
F +49.541.572660
info@architekci.info
www.architekci.info

→ 34

Kengo Kuma & Associates

2-24-8 Minamiaoyama Minatoku
Tokyo 107-0062 (Japan)
T +81.3.34017721
F +81.3.34017778
kuma@ba2.so-net.ne.jp
www.kkaa.co.jp

→ 28

Labics

Via dei Magazzini Generali, 16
00154 Rome (Italy)
T +39.06.57288049
F +39.06.57137808
info@labics.it
www.labics.it

→ 32

Lapointe Architects

10 Saint Mary Street, Suite 606
Toronto, ON M4Y1P9 (Canada)
T +1.416.9646641
F +1.416.9646643
info@lapointe-arch.com
www.lapointe-arch.com

→ 156

LEHRER + GANGI DESIGN + BUILD

2140 Hyperion Avenue, Silverlake
Los Angeles, CA 90027-4708 (USA)
T +1.323.6644747
F +1.323.6643566
e. michael@lehrerarchitects.com
www.lehrerarchitects.com

→366

Lindsay Johnston Architect

16 Milson's Passage, Hawkesbury River
via Brooklyn, NSW 2083 (Australia)
T +61.2.99851262
F +61.2.99851264
lindsay@rivertime.org
www.rivertime.org

→86

Line and Space, LLC

627 E. Speedway Boulevard
Tucson, AZ 85705 (USA)
T +1.520.6231313
F +1.520.6231303
studio627@lineandspace.com
www.lineandspace.com

→ 218

Lord, Aeck & Sargent

213 South Ashley Street, Suite 200
Ann Arbor, MI 48104 (USA)
T +1.877.9291400
F +1.877.9291401
info@lasarchitects.com
www.lordaecksargent.com

→ 354

conrad lutz architecte sàrl

14, rue Jean Prouvé
1762 Givisiez (Switzerland)
T +41.26.4697400
F +41.26.4697409
office@lutz-architecte.ch
www.lutz-architecte.ch

→ 168

Prof. Christoph Mäckler Architekten

Platz der Republik 6
60325 Frankfurt / Main (Germany)
T +49.69.50508000
F +49.69.505080060
chm@chm.de
www.chm.de

→ 330

MEIXNER-SCHLÜTER-WENDT Architekten

Fischerfeldstraße 13
60311 Frankfurt / Main (Germany)
T +49.69.2102860
F +49.69.21028620
info@meixner-schlueter-wendt.de
www.meixner-schlueter-wendt.de

→ 66

Modostudio

Via Amerigo Vespucci, 24
00153 Rome (Italy)
T +39.06.87908809
F +39.06.87908809
info@modostudio.eu
www.modostudio.eu

→ 416

Paul Morgan Architects

221 Queen Street, Level 10
Melbourne, VIC 3000 (Australia)
T +61.3.96003253
F +61.3.96025673
office@paulmorganarchitects.com
www.paulmorganarchitects.com

→ 18

MURPHY/JAHN

35 East Wacker Drive, 3rd Floor
Chicago, IL 60601 (USA)
T +1.312.4277300
F +1.312.3320274
info@murphyjahn.com
www.murphyjahn.com

→ 342

Ateliers Jean Nouvel

10, cité d'Angoulême
75011 Paris (France)
T +33.1.49238383
F +33.1.43148110
info@jeannouvel.fr
www.jeannouvel.fr

→ 126

Onix

P.O. Box 474
9700 AL Groningen (The Netherlands)
T +31.50.5290252
F +31.50.5290282
info@onix.nl
www.onix.nl

→ 250

Opus Architekten BDA

Ploenniesstraße 14–16
64289 Darmstadt (Germany)
T +49.6151.96490
F +49.6151.964930
mail@opus-architekten.de
www.opus-architekten.de

→ 100

PAUAT Architekten

Bernardingasse 14
4600 Wels (Austria)
T +43.7242.796600
F +43.7242.7966060
office@pau.at
www.pau.at

→ 222

perraudinarchitectes

16, rue Jacques Imbert Colomès
69001 Lyon (France)
T +33.4.72109640
T +33.4.72109649
perraudinarchitectes@wanadoo.fr
www.perraudinarchitectes.com

→ 254

pfeifer. kuhn. architekten

Gartenstraße 19
79098 Freiburg (Germany)
T +49.761.2967690
F +49.761.29676920
architekten@pfeifer-kuhn.de
www.pfeifer-kuhn.de

→ 160, 172

Renzo Piano Building Workshop

Via Rubens, 29
16158 Genova (Italy)
T +39.010.61711
F +39.010.6171350
italy@rpbw.com
www.rpbw.r.ui-pro.com

→ 370

Antoine Predock, Architect

300 12th Street
Albuquerque, NM 87102 (USA)
T +1.505.8437390
F +1.505.2436254
studio@apredock.com
www.predock.com

→ **186**

Pugh + Scarpa Architects, Inc.

2525 Michigan Avenue, Building F1
Santa Monica, CA 90404 (USA)
T +1.310.8280226
F +1.310.4539606
info@pugh-scarpa.com
www.pugh-scarpa.com

→ **40**

RADAarchitects

233 North Michigan Avenue, Suite 2320
Chicago, IL 60601 (USA)
T +1.312.8561970
F +1.312.8651978
contact@rada-arch.com
www.rada-arch.com

→ **164**

Silvio Rech and Lesley Carstens Architects

32b Pallinghurst Road
Westcliff 2193 (South Africa)
T +27.11.486-1525
adventarch@mweb.co.za

→ **422**

Riepl Riepl Architekten

Ok-Platz 1a / Dametzstraße 38
4020 Linz (Austria)
T +43.732.782300
F +43.732.78230019
arch@rieplriepl.com
www.rieplriepl.com

→**182**

Rios Clementi Hale Studios

639 N Larchmont Boulevard
Los Angeles, CA 90004 (USA)
T +1.323.7851800
F +1.323.7851801
www.rchstudios.com

→ **292**

Philippe Samyn and Partners, architects & engineers

1537, chaussée de Waterloo
1180 Brussels (Belgium)
T +32.2.3749060
F +32.2.3747550
sai@samynandpartners.be
www.samynandpartners.be

→ **194**

sander architects, LLC

2524 Lincoln Boulevard
Venice, CA 90291 (USA)
T +1.310.8220300
F +1.310.8220900
info@sander-architects.com
www.sander-architects.com

→ **44, 70**

sauerbruch hutton

Lehrter Straße 57
10557 Berlin (Germany)
T +49.30.3978210
F +49.30.397821920
mail@sauerbruchhutton.com
www.sauerbruchhutton.com

→ **324**

Todd Saunders

Vestre torggate 22
5015 Bergen (Norway)
T +47.55.368506
F +47.97.525761
post@saunders.no
www.saunders.no

→ **90**

SFA Simon Freie Architekten

Hackstraße 20
70190 Stuttgart (Germany)
T +49.711.6152275
F +49.711.6152283
simon-freie-architekten@email.de
www.simon-freie-architekten.de

Shubin + Donaldson Architects, Inc.

1 North Calle Cesar Chavez, Suite 200
Santa Barbara, CA 93103 (USA)
T +1.805.9662802
F +1.805.9663002
www.sandarc.com

SITE – Sculpture In The Environment

25 Maiden Lane
New York City, NY 10038-4008 (USA)
T +1.212.2850120
F +1.212.2850125
Info@SITEnewyork.com
www.siteenvirodesign.com

SJB Architects

25 Coventry Street, Southbank
Melbourne, VIC 3006 (Australia)
T +61.3.96996688
F +61.3.96966234
architects@sjb.com.au
www.sjb.com.au

Skidmore, Owings & Merril LLP

One Front Street, Suite 2400
San Francisco, CA 94111 (USA)
T +1.415.9811555
F +1.415.3983214
somsanfrancisco@som.com
www.som.com

SMAQ – architecture urbanism research

C. Beersmanstraat 5D
3025 EA Rotterdam (The Netherlands)
T +31.10.4520032
F +31.842.221917
mail@smaq.net
www.smaq.net

Michael Sorkin Studio

180 Varick Street, Suite 930
New York City, NY 10014 (USA)
T +1.212.6279120
F +1.212.6279125
sorkin@thing.net
www.sorkinstudio.com

Studio Granda

Smiðjustígur 11b
Reykjavík IS101 (Iceland)
T +354.562.2661
F +354.552.6626
studiogranda@studiogranda.is
www.studiogranda.is

TEAM0708 Építész Ltd.

Királyi Pál u. 4.
1053 Budapest (Hungary)
T +36.1.2674243
F +36.1.2674243
email@team0708.hu
www.team0708.hu

Jens J. Ternes Architekt BDA, Architekten + Ingenieure

Schulgasse 2
56073 Koblenz (Germany)
T +49.261.9883880
F +49.261.98838888
info@architektternes.de
www.architektternes.de

Michael Tribus Architecture

Via Bersaglio, 9/1
39011 Lana (Italy)
T +39.0473.550681
F +39.0473.554175
mail@michaeltribus.com
www.michaeltribus.com

Turf Design Studio

P.O. Box 419
Cronulla, NSW 2230 (Australia)
T +61.2.95273380
F +61.2.95272307
sydney@turfdesign.com
www.turfdesign.com

→ **38**

Valode et Pistre architectes

115, rue du Bac
75007 Paris (France)
T +33.1.53632200
F +33.1.53632209
info@v-p.com
www.valode-et-pistre.com

→ **412**

VJAA

400 1st Avenue North, Suite 410
Minneapolis, MN 55401-1351 (USA)
T +1.612.8726370
F +1.612.8726380
e-mail@vjaa.com
www.vjaa.com

→ **130**

X ARCHITECTS

Dubai Healthcare City (DHCC), Building No. 47, Offices
105 & 106, P.O.Box 111559
Dubai (U.A.E.)
T +97.14.4298309
F +97.14.4298308
xarc@x-architects.com
www.x-architects.com

→ **392**

XRANGE

6F, 51 Heng Yang Road
Taipei 100 (Taiwan)
T +886.2.23832003
F +886.2.23316460
xrange@xrange.net
www.xrange.net

→ **410**

All other pictures, especially portraits and plans, were made available by the architects.

Cover front: Sharon Risedorph

Cover back (left and right): Michael Moran Studio

IMPRINT

The Deutsche Bibliothek is registering this publication in
the Deutsche Nationalbibliographie; detailed bibliographi-
cal information can be found on the Internet at http://
dnb.ddb.de

ISBN 978-3-03768-010-0

© 2009 by Braun Publishing AG
www.braun-publishing.ch

2nd edition 2010

Editorial staff: Marek Heinel, Natascha Saupe
Translation: Alice Bayandin
Graphic concept: ON Grafik | Tom Wibberenz
Layout: Natascha Saupe
Reproduction: Bild1Druck GmbH, Berlin